DON'T LOSE IT

7 Smart Legal Moves to
Secure Your Financial Fortress

~

Toni Moore, ESQ, LLM, CEBS

Table of Contents

Introduction

B eing an entrepreneur is a thrilling adventure, but it can turn into a disaster if you're not legally and financially protected. Too many business owners repeat the same expensive mistakes because they don't have the right tools in place to secure their success. And do you know why? Because they're too busy "winging it" and thinking they'll figure it out as they go. Spoiler alert: That's not a strategy—that's a recipe for chaos!

Let's get real for a second: Would you jump out of a plane without a parachute? I hope you figure out how to land on the way down. Of course not. But somehow, entrepreneurs think they can launch a business with no legal safety net and expect it to stay intact magically. Well, here's the hard truth—when you run a business without a legal plan, it's not a question of if something will go wrong; it's a matter of when. Skipping the legal prep is like playing Jenga with your business, just waiting for one wrong move to send it all crashing down. Sure, it's easy to get caught up in the excitement of scaling, growing, and making money—but what good is all that hustle if one legal misstep can wipe out everything you've built? You wouldn't drive a car without insurance or leave your front door wide open for anyone to walk in, right? Yet somehow, people convince themselves that running a business without the proper protection is totally fine. Well, newsflash—it's not.

One lawsuit, one partnership gone wrong, one bad contract, and suddenly, you're in the kind of mess that even the best public relations (PR) advisor/team can't spin you out of. You've worked too hard to let all of it go up in flames because of something you could've prevented. And because of this, you should not fly by the seat of your pants. What I know for sure is that it's only a matter of time before the "winging it" mentality turns into a very expensive litigation and/or lawsuit. And who has time for that? That's why you need to build your financial fortress and create legal chess strategies so that no one can checkmate on your assets.

As a serial entrepreneur and creative myself, I know all about building intellectual property—trust me, I've got ideas for days! But as a lawyer? Oh, I definitely know that if I don't lock it down, one wrong move could wipe it all out faster than you can say, "Oops." When things go wrong in business, they don't just go wrong—they really go wrong. And you do not want to be caught without a backup plan! Litigation, lawyers, and the legal process are expensive. That's why you've got to have your legal and financial fortress on lock, so nothing and no one messes with your legacy!

WHAT IS A FINANCIAL FORTRESS?

So happy you asked!

Building a financial fortress isn't just about keeping the bad stuff out—it's about creating a solid structure that can withstand anything life throws your way. Think of your business like a house. If the foundation is shaky, the first storm that hits could leave it in shambles, right? You're not trying to build some flimsy tent; you want a castle, something that stands strong through every storm, challenge, and curveball. But here's the thing: most entrepreneurs build their businesses without a solid legal and financial foundation and wonder why everything falls apart when they hit a rough patch. That's where your financial fortress comes in. The game plan ensures that no matter what happens—whether it's a legal issue, an economic downturn, or an unexpected business hiccup—your business is protected and set up to grow and create long-lasting wealth.

So, What Does a Financial Fortress Look Like?

> ➤ **Legal Armor**: First, let's discuss your legal armor. This is your first line of defense, darling. Contracts, intellectual property protection, proper business formation—this is where you lock it down tighter than your grandma's secret recipe. You wouldn't run a coaching business without a rock-solid contract for clients, right? Or how about developing a killer course only to find someone else is cashing in on your hard work because you didn't secure the trademark? Honey, building your legal armor prevents these disasters and keeps your assets safe.

> ➤ **Tax Strategy**: Let's get real; taxes are like that annoying ex who just won't quit. But instead of waiting for the IRS to show up with a bill that makes your heart drop, you can build a tax strategy that helps you keep more of your hard-earned cash. We're discussing setting up the right entity structure, maximizing deductions, and planning for tax-deferred accounts. A strong tax strategy is like

having a moat around your financial fortress—it keeps those pesky losses at bay.

➢ **Asset Protection**: Have you ever heard the saying, "Don't put all your eggs in one basket?" In business, that rule is a total must. Protecting your assets from your business liabilities is crucial. You don't want a lawsuit to knock on your door, and suddenly, you're on the line for your savings, home, or retirement funds. You want to ensure your assets are secure and off-limits from being lost, diminished, or stolen. And the only way to ensure your treasures are off-limits is to build your fortress correctly.

➢ **Diversified Revenue Streams**: Another key pillar of a financial fortress? Multiple ways to make money! If one stream dries up, you've got others to keep you afloat. So, if you're a consultant, don't just sit back and wait for clients—create a digital course, write a book, or license your intellectual property to generate passive income. Diversification means that when one storm tries to remove a section of your business, it doesn't bring the whole house crashing down.

➢ **Recession-Proof Planning**: Now we're getting to the cherry on top of your fortress—making sure your business can survive tough times and thrive in them. We're talking about creating products or services that people need no matter what. If your business offers solutions that help other businesses save money or boost efficiency, guess what? You're going to stay in demand when times get tough. You're not just preparing for the good times; you're building your fortress to withstand the lean times, too.

The bottom line is that your financial fortress is all about protection and growth. It's not just a nice-to-have—turning your entrepreneurial dream into long-lasting wealth is essential. Without these protections, you're leaving yourself vulnerable to all sorts of risks that can wipe out everything you've worked for. But when your financial fortress is solid? You're not just surviving the storms—thriving, growing, and building lasting wealth.

WHAT IS WEALTH BUILDING?

Before I became the Legal Deeva, I proudly wore the title of Wealth-Building Lawyer, and let me tell you, there's a reason for that! One of my favorite mantras is: "Turn your LLCs into long-lasting currency." And the best way to do that? By leveraging what I call the "Trifecta of Financial Success." What's that, you ask? It's a powerhouse combo of a holding company, a business entity, and a trust—all harmoniously working together to build and protect your legacy. In other words, it's the sheer power of understanding how to leverage your intellectual property. It's all about transforming your genius into a brand that commands respect and generates revenue. When you start landing sponsorships, licensing deals, or joint ventures, you're not just turning knowledge into a bankable asset; you're stacking your financial deck in your favor! You can set aside up to $56,000 in retirement plans alone and then take that cash and invest it in more assets like real estate or even a nonprofit. You're not just building wealth for today; you're paving the way for your family's financial future for generations to come.

Wealth-building for an entrepreneur is much like playing chess. Every move counts, darling! If you're strategic, you're not just moving pieces but positioning yourself to win big. Beyoncé famously said, "My Momma, My Lawyer, My Shield!" and she knew exactly what she was talking about. She recognizes that her lawyer is critical in protecting her wealth and legacy. Lawyers like me are similar to knights in shining armor—shielding your assets, defending your brand, and ensuring that nobody checkmates your financial future. When you're building wealth through entrepreneurship, you're creating streams of income that go far beyond a paycheck. Let's keep it real: working for someone else means Uncle Sam gets a hefty slice of that pie, leaving you to scrape by on the crumbs. But when you own a business—whether it's a full-time gig or a fabulous side hustle—you're the one calling the shots. And even if you take a hit in your side hustle, that loss can help reduce your tax bill.

I've seen way too many people pour their hard-earned cash into the stock market, mutual funds, or 401(k)s, hoping for a decent return, only to be let down by sluggish growth and sky-high fees. But imagine flipping the script! What if you turned your brilliance into something tangible? What if you crafted a proprietary framework, developed a course, wrote a book, or created a video library? Now, we're talking real assets—assets that can generate revenue, get licensed, and ultimately be passed down to your family through a trust. That's the secret sauce for creating long-lasting currency! Let's look at the celebrities we adore.

They're not merely cashing checks from one source; they've got trademarks, real estate, intellectual property, and multiple businesses working together like a well-oiled machine. Take Taylor Swift, for instance. She holds over three hundred (300) trademarks, but here's the kicker—they're not in her personal name. Nope, they're tucked away in her holding company. That's the game, darling! Wealthy individuals build layers of protection around their assets, so if one venture hits a bump in the road, the rest of their empire stays intact.

So, when discussing smart legal moves, I'm not just throwing around legal jargon. I'm handing you the blueprint to build a financial fortress that stands the test of time. Your LLC can be the solid foundation, but the strategy—the chess moves—transforms it into long-lasting currency. This ensures that you protect your assets from loss, bankruptcy, or even someone trying to snatch away what's rightfully yours. Because, to be honest, it's about legally building your empire by creating a business that not only builds, monetizes, and protects your intellectual property but also secures your family's future.

WHY "DON'T LOSE IT?"

If you're hustling to build a thriving business, the last thing you want is to watch it collapse like a house of cards because you overlooked some essential legal steps. That's precisely why I wrote, "DON'T LOSE IT." With over 20 years as a litigator and now specializing in estate planning, business law, and taxation, I'm here to tell you that I've seen it all. I've witnessed the fallout from entrepreneurs who didn't take these steps seriously, and I don't want that to be you!

This isn't just theory; this is battle-tested wisdom designed to give you the upper hand. You'll walk away feeling like a legal superhero, armed with the knowledge to safeguard your assets and keep the wolves at bay. Whether it's ensuring that your intellectual property is protected or that your business structure is solid enough to withstand any storm, I'm committed to offering you the tools to prevent and protect your legacies and lifestyles.

This book is your ultimate legal playbook, designed to guide you through the crucial steps every entrepreneur needs to consider. I'm serving up the seven smart legal moves every entrepreneur should be making, and trust me, you don't want to miss them. We'll explore how to craft airtight contracts, protect intellectual property, and set up a tax strategy that leaves more cash in your pocket and less in Uncle Sam's. And we're not stopping there! We'll dive into asset protection strategies that ensure your hard work stays yours, even when life throws those curveballs.

Each chapter is packed with juicy insights and practical tips to implement immediately. I'm not just throwing random legal jargon your way; I'm breaking it down into bite-sized pieces that are easy to digest (and even easier to act on). Expect real-life examples, relatable anecdotes, and a little sass to keep things lively! You'll see how other entrepreneurs have dodged disasters and secured their wealth, and you'll be inspired to do the same.

By the end of this book, you'll have a treasure chest of tools that will educate and empower you to protect your legacy, lifestyle, and everything in between. You'll grasp the importance of each legal move and feel confident enough to implement them. So, get ready to stop the cycle of "I wish I had known that" or "calling the attorney during the lawsuit" and start confidently living your entrepreneurial dreams! By turning that last page, you won't just understand the importance of legal protections; you'll be ready to build your financial fortress powerfully, profitably, and purposefully. You'll have a clear blueprint that shows you how to secure your wealth and paves the way for growth. This book is for entrepreneurs ready to make smart legal moves and informed decisions to keep their businesses flourishing and their financial futures profitable.

GET READY!!!!! GET READY!!!

If you're a millionaire, a thousandaire, or just scraping by with a couple hundred bucks, listen up: don't sacrifice your success on the altar of ignorance regarding the law and entrepreneurship. Sure, law can be, at times, a jealous mistress—demanding attention and commitment—but ignoring her could cost you far more than a few late-night phone calls. Choosing to sidestep legal matters because you think they're "not for you" is like inviting disaster into your life. Whether you're raking in the big bucks or just starting your financial journey, the consequences of legal neglect can be catastrophic. A single lawsuit, a forgotten compliance requirement, or even a misunderstood regulation can quickly turn your financial fortress into a house of cards.

So why risk it? Embrace the law! Educate yourself, invest in legal advice, and treat your legal obligations with the seriousness they deserve. It's not about getting "in bed" with the law; it's about creating a partnership that protects your interests and paves the way for your success. After all, a little diligence now can save you a world of headaches—

and a lot of money—down the road. Don't be the entrepreneur who says, "I'll deal with it later." Take the leap and make legal a part of your team so you Don't LOSE everything you have built!

Why Do You Need to Honor the Legal Side of Business?

I know that for many, law isn't the most thrilling topic in the world. It's often seen as a dry, tedious subject, something we're vaguely aware of but don't truly dive into until we're neck-deep in a legal problem. Most of us were raised to know some aspects of law, but let's be honest—half of us don't really get invested until we absolutely need it. But here's a little secret: law isn't just a bunch of dusty old rules confined to ancient times. Nope! It's the very backbone of society, the glue that keeps everything from falling apart, and the essential playbook for navigating the chaotic journey of life and business. So, why should you care? Because law is intricately tied to your freedom, access, and lifestyle. It lays the groundwork for the rights you claim in both your personal life and your entrepreneurial endeavors. Think about it: the law protects your ability to pursue happiness, safeguard your property, and maintain your intellectual creations. It's the framework that allows you to thrive, innovate, and even argue for what's yours. Without an understanding of the law, you risk losing your footing in a world where boundaries and rights can quickly blur. Whether you're signing contracts, launching a new product, or simply trying to navigate the intricacies of daily life, knowing the law empowers you to stand your ground and make informed decisions. It's your shield against injustice, your guide through the maze of regulations, and your ally in the fight for fairness.

WHAT IS LAW? & WHY DO WE HAVE TO FOLLOW IT IN BUSINESS?

At its core, law is the set of rules and guidelines that govern society. Think of it as the ultimate rulebook for life, a manual designed to keep everything in order and ensure that we all play nice. Without law, we'd be living in a chaotic free-for-all where everyone does whatever they please, and trust me, that's a recipe for disaster. I always say that Law is like a jealous mistress. She might not be the most glamorous of companions but trust me; when she feels disrespected or neglected, her wrath will explode. You don't want to be caught in the fallout when she decides to unleash her fury, leaving everyone in her path scrambling to pick up the pieces and bowing down to her demands. So, give her the attention she deserves—because if you don't, you'll find out just how fierce she can be!

Now, when it comes to business, the law is much like your best friend, and your worst nightmare all rolled into one. It's what allows you to protect your brilliant ideas, ensures fair play in the marketplace, and gives you the power to defend your rights if someone tries to mess with your hustle. But it also means you have to follow a lot of rules. Yes, that's right—rules. From contracts to compliance, intellectual property to employment laws, you need to be aware of a smorgasbord of legal obligations. And let's be honest, nobody likes reading the fine print. But why bother?

Because following the law isn't just about avoiding fines or staying out of jail; it's about building a solid foundation for your business.

When you adhere to the law, you establish trust with your customers, investors, and partners. You're saying, "Hey, I play by the rules, and you can count on me!" This trust is invaluable and can set you apart in a crowded marketplace. Plus, having a grasp on legal matters can save you from some serious headaches down the line. Imagine launching your dream business only to discover you've accidentally infringed on someone's trademark or violated a contract. Yikes! Not only can that lead to costly legal battles, but it can also tarnish your reputation and jeopardize your hard-earned success.

So, while it may feel tedious to incorporate legal into your business or life, it's a necessary evil. It's like wearing a seatbelt in a car—you might find it annoying, but it's there to protect you when things go south. And trust me, when the legal stakes are high, you'll be grateful for that safety net. So embrace the law as your ally, learn the ropes, and let it guide you toward building a thriving, reputable business. Because in the end, a savvy business owner knows that understanding and respecting the law isn't just a choice—it's a game-changer! And just so you understand why this is a team member you need, here are some legal examples that illustrate the importance of law in business, so you don't lose it.

- o **Contracts** ~ Example: A startup enters into a contract with a supplier for raw materials. The contract specifies delivery dates, payment terms, and quality standards. If the supplier fails to deliver on time, the startup can sue for breach of contract to seek damages or enforce compliance. This underscores the importance of having solid contractual agreements in place to protect business interests.

- **Intellectual Property (IP) Rights** ~ Example: A tech company develops a groundbreaking software application. By trademarking its name and patenting its technology, the company protects its IP from competitors who might want to replicate its innovations. If another company uses the software without permission, the original company can file a lawsuit for infringement, ensuring that its hard work is safeguarded.

- **Employment Law** ~ Example: A business hires an employee and fails to comply with labor laws regarding wages, overtime, and working conditions. If the employee files a complaint, the business could face fines and lawsuits. Understanding employment law helps businesses create fair policies, reduce turnover, and avoid legal disputes.

- **Consumer Protection Laws** ~ Example: A food company markets a product as "organic" without proper certification. If consumers discover that the product does not meet organic standards, they can file lawsuits for false advertising. Adhering to consumer protection laws helps businesses maintain credibility and avoid damaging legal issues.

- **Data Protection and Privacy Laws** ~ Example: An e-commerce site collects customer data but fails to comply with regulations like the General Data

Protection Regulation (GDPR). If a customer's data is breached and the company did not follow proper protocols, it could face hefty fines and loss of consumer trust. Businesses must understand data protection laws to safeguard customer information and avoid liability.

- o **Business Licenses and Permits** ~ Example: A restaurant opens without obtaining the necessary health permits. During a surprise inspection, authorities shut down the restaurant, leading to financial losses and damage to reputation. Complying with local regulations and obtaining the required licenses ensures smooth operations and legal protection.

- o **Franchise Agreements** ~ Example: A franchisee signs an agreement to operate a fast-food restaurant. The agreement outlines fees, operational procedures, and branding guidelines. If the franchisee violates these terms, the franchisor can terminate the agreement, protecting the brand's integrity. Understanding franchise law is crucial for both franchisors and franchisees to navigate their rights and responsibilities.

- o **Tax Compliance** ~ Example: A business fails to pay its taxes and faces penalties from the IRS. Not only could it incur hefty fines, but it could also jeopardize its operations and reputation. Understanding tax law and staying compliant is essential for sustainable business practices.

These examples highlight the critical role of law in protecting your business, maintaining ethical standards, and ensuring long-term success. Ignoring legal considerations can lead to costly mistakes, while a proactive approach to legal matters helps safeguard your brand and legacy.

COMPLIANCE: BECAUSE NOBODY LIKES A RULE-BREAKER

When you hear the word "compliance," does your mind start wandering to a snooze-fest of regulations and rule books? I get it; for many entrepreneurs, compliance feels like a necessary evil, like the broccoli on your plate that you have to eat before you can get to dessert. But here's the juicy truth: compliance isn't just some boring, stuffy obligation—it's your golden ticket to success! Think of compliance as your business's best friend. It's the secret sauce that not only keeps you out of hot water but also helps you build a brand that customers can trust. Without compliance, you're walking a tightrope without a safety net, one misstep away from disaster. Ignoring it? Well, that's like throwing caution to the wind and hoping for the best—bold, but not very smart!

So why should you care about compliance? Because it's more than just following the rules; it's about laying a solid foundation for your business that can withstand the storms of legal challenges, reputational risks, and operational hiccups. It's about ensuring that your hard work pays off and that your legacy remains intact. You wouldn't build a house without a solid foundation, would you? So why would you build a business without compliance?

The very first step on your compliance journey is to become well-acquainted with the laws and regulations that apply to your business. This isn't just a casual glance; it requires digging deep into the legal framework governing your industry. Whether it's federal, state, or local laws, you need to know what's what. Don't hesitate to consult with legal experts who can provide clarity on any gray areas. Trust me, understanding the legal landscape can save you from headaches—and potential lawsuits—down the line. Think of it as the groundwork for building a skyscraper: you need a solid foundation before you can reach for the stars. Once you've got the legal know-how under your belt, it's time to put that knowledge into action by establishing clear policies and procedures. This step is critical! Outline how your business will comply with relevant laws by creating documents such as employee handbooks, codes of conduct, data protection policies, and financial protocols. These aren't just fancy pieces of paper; they are the blueprints for your organization's integrity. Ensure that these documents are easily accessible to all employees so everyone knows the rules of the game. A well-informed team is a compliant team, and clear guidelines pave the way for smooth operations.

Compliance isn't a one-and-done deal; it's an ongoing effort that requires continuous education and reinforcement. Regularly train your staff on compliance policies and legal requirements to keep them in the know. Make it a priority to educate your team about the importance of compliance and their individual roles in maintaining it. Host workshops, seminars, or even casual lunch-and-learns. The goal is to create a culture where compliance is ingrained in your company's DNA. After all, the more your employees understand compliance, the more likely they are to spot potential issues before they escalate.

Speaking of potential issues, conducting periodic compliance audits is essential for assessing your adherence to laws and internal policies. This proactive approach allows you to identify any areas of concern before they snowball into significant problems. Think of it as a routine health check-up for your business; you want to catch any irregularities before they lead to a crisis. Use these audits as opportunities to improve your compliance programs continuously. It's all about fine-tuning your operations and ensuring that you're not just following the rules but thriving under them. Because in the fast-paced world of business, laws and regulations can change more often than your favorite social media trend. That's why it's crucial to stay informed about any legal developments that may impact your industry. Subscribe to industry newsletters, join professional organizations, or regularly consult with legal counsel to keep your knowledge up to date.

Remember, ignorance is not bliss when it comes to legal or compliance; it's a potential ticket to disaster. The more informed you are, the better equipped you'll be to adapt and pivot as needed. Now, I know what you might be thinking: "Toni, why do I need all this for my 'small business?" "I don't even know if I'm going to be in business that long. Is this even worth it?" Well, let me give you a little wake-up call. Ignoring compliance and the law is like playing with fire—only, instead of a cozy campfire, you're sitting on a volcano about to erupt! Trust me, you don't want to be caught in the middle of that disaster zone. Didn't I warn you before that the law is like a "jealous mistress?" She'll come knocking when you least expect it, and when she does, she's not interested in your excuses or plans to "see how it goes." So, before you shrug off compliance as just another annoying obligation, think again! The consequences of negligence will turn your business dreams into a cautionary tale faster than you can say "lawsuit."

So, do you get why I'm always strutting my stuff on social media, hopping on stages, hitting up conferences, and doing media interviews to talk legal and get your business in order? It's not just for kicks! Ignoring your legal obligations is like inviting disaster over for tea. Not only will she snatch your business right out from under you, but she'll also drain your financial fortress with a barrage of fees and lawsuits and maybe even take a few swipes at your sanity and freedom. If you've never been sued, summoned, or, heaven forbid, imprisoned, let me tell you: mishandling your business is NOT the time to learn those hard lessons. So, let's get it together and avoid turning your dreams into a legal nightmare! But if you are still not convinced, let's review some of the issues you can face by "riding dirty" in these business streets.

First off, let's talk about legal penalties. Non-compliance is like waving a big red flag in front of the law, and trust me, the last thing you want is to attract attention from the legal eagles. Depending on the severity of your violation, you could be staring down the barrel of hefty fines, penalties, or even criminal charges. Yes, you heard that right—criminal charges. These costs can drain your financial resources faster than a celebrity on a shopping spree, leaving your bottom line looking a whole lot thinner. If you think you can operate under the radar, think again. Regulatory bodies can decide to revoke your business licenses or permits if you fail to comply with the laws governing your industry. That's right; they can effectively hit the "pause" button on your operations, leaving you twiddling your thumbs while your competition zooms ahead. Talk about a serious blow to your hustle! And let's not forget about your brand's reputation. Non-compliance can be a PR nightmare. Imagine your loyal customers finding out that your business isn't playing by the rules—trust me, they'll be out the door faster than you can say "compliance issues." When customers lose faith in your ability to do business ethically, it can lead to decreased sales, a significant drop in your customer base, and a major uphill battle when it comes to attracting new clients. Your brand becomes synonymous with "no thanks," and that's not the kind of legacy anyone wants to leave behind.

Once your business gets flagged for non-compliance, you can expect to find yourself under a magnifying glass. Increased scrutiny from regulators, customers, and even competitors can feel like being trapped in a reality show that you never signed up for. Your every move will be monitored, and the pressure can lead to further legal complications and operational headaches. Let's be real—who needs that kind of stress when you're just trying to run a successful business? And if you think that's the end of your troubles, think again. Non-compliance can open the floodgates to litigation risks, making you a prime target for lawsuits from customers, employees, or even competitors looking to take you down a notch. Legal battles can drag on for ages, costing you a fortune in legal fees and diverting your focus from growing your business. You'll be stuck playing defense instead of offense, and nobody wants that.

So, as tempting as it may be to cut corners or ignore the rules, remember that the fallout from non-compliance is far more costly than doing things the right way from the get-go. In the world of business, compliance isn't just a checkbox—it's your lifeline. So, honor the law, protect your brand, and keep your business thriving!

WHY YOU SHOULD ADD A LAWYER TO YOUR TEAM?

How many of you have actually retained an attorney for your business? For those of you who said yes, kudos! You're strutting your stuff like the savvy bosses you are! But for those of you who said no? Honey, that's not just a missed opportunity; it's like walking a tightrope without a safety net—risky and downright foolish! Look, when you're running a business, you're not just selling products or services; you're playing a game of chess with legal intricacies lurking at every corner. You need a skilled strategist—your attorney—by your side to navigate the potential minefields of compliance, contracts, and legal obligations. Ignoring this crucial step is like bringing a butter knife to a gunfight; it's just not smart!

Now, think about the other professionals you might already have on your team. Maybe you've got an accountant managing your books because you know that numbers don't lie, and financial missteps can spell tax issues and audits. Or perhaps you've hired a social media manager to boost your online presence because you understand the importance of branding and audience engagement in today's digital age. So why, oh why, would you skimp on legal support when those same risks loom around every corner? You wouldn't let your accountant handle your social media strategy, right? That's because each expert brings specialized knowledge to the table. Similarly, an attorney understands the ins and outs of legal regulations, contracts, and compliance that you might not even know exist! They'll help you dodge legal landmines, ensuring you don't get into any trouble that could derail your hard-earned success. Think about it this way: every time you enter a contract, hire an employee, or even post something on social media, there are legal implications. Do you really want to be the entrepreneur who finds out the hard way that you violated a regulation? Or worse, gets slapped with a lawsuit that could've been avoided with a little foresight? No, thank you!

Having a lawyer on your team not only helps you dodge those legal issues but also sends a message that you mean business—literally! It shows investors, partners, and customers that you're serious about protecting your brand and your assets. Plus, they can help you craft agreements, speak on your behalf, protect your assets, and keep your interests safeguarded while you focus on growing your empire. As a lawyer and business owner, don't wait until you're knee-deep in a legal threat or trouble to make a smart legal move. Be proactive and have the #LegalDeeva in your corner. Trust me; your faith, family, and funds will thank you for it!

Legal Move #1: Formalize Your Business

Legally formalizing your business is not just about compliance, but more about asset protection while securing your financial future through entrepreneurship
— Toni Moore

T he first smart legal move to secure your generational wealth-building legacy is to formalize your business. Now, before you roll your eyes and think, "Ugh, more paperwork," let me set the record straight: formalizing your business isn't just about filling out forms; it's about laying the foundation for a legacy that will stand the test of time. When you create a business that generates income, you're planting the seeds for your wealth-building future. It's like watering a money tree—you want it to grow big and strong, not shrivel up and die because you didn't take the necessary steps to nurture it. Plus, let's be real: who doesn't want to leave a lasting impact on the world while raking in the profits?

But hold on! This isn't a one-size-fits-all situation, darling. Each entrepreneur's journey is unique, and the last thing you want is to shoehorn your dreams into a cookie-cutter strategy. It's time to get savvy and appreciate the various types of business entities out there because they can make or break your wealth-building efforts. Whether you're eyeing a sole proprietorship for that solo hustle, an LLC for the perfect blend of protection and flexibility, or a corporation to attract big-time investors, choosing the right structure is crucial for maximizing your potential and protecting your assets. Think of it as finding the perfect outfit for your business—something that fits just right and makes you feel fabulous! So, let's roll up those sleeves and dive into the exciting world of business entities because your legacy deserves nothing less than the best!

Sole Proprietor

Let's break it down: the sole proprietor structure is like the starter kit of business ownership. It's simple, cheap, and practically no paperwork. The minute you start selling anything—whether it's a product or a service—you're automatically the sole proprietor. You don't need a lawyer, a board meeting, or even a change of address. You can operate under your own name or a business name you make up on the spot. And just like that, you've got the power to hire, fire, and make money by offering your services. But—and here's the thing—being a sole proprietor comes with its own set of risks. You've got complete control, but that also means complete responsibility. If something goes wrong, like if you find yourself in hot water with regulators, in a dispute with a client, or slapped with a lawsuit, it's not just your business on the line.

The biggest downside to being a sole proprietor is that your liability is unlimited. That means, if you lose in court or face heavy fines, they don't just come after your business bank account—they can also come after your personal assets. Your home, car, savings, and anything else under your name could be at risk. In other words, you're not just risking your business—you're risking everything you personally own. So, while the sole proprietorship may be an easy and attractive option for getting started, it's important to weigh that against the personal exposure it brings. Sure, it's your business, and you can run it exactly how you see fit, but if something goes wrong, the financial fallout could follow you right into your personal life.

LIMITED LIABILITY COMPANY

Alright, now let's talk about the Limited Liability Company or LLC, and why it's one of the slickest ways to flex your entrepreneurial muscle. If the sole proprietorship is like diving into the deep end alone, the LLC is like swimming with floaties on—still freedom, but with some serious protection. Here's the deal: you can fly solo with your LLC as the lone member or gather a group of fellow business bosses to create a multi-member LLC. If you're teaming up, it's kind of like being in a business marriage. You and your partners will have to set some ground rules—who gets to vote on decisions, who's bringing what to the table, how you'll divvy up the profits, and, oh yeah, what happens if someone decides to peace out. It's like building a business prenup, and trust me, you'll be glad you did.

Now, let's talk structure. You can run your LLC as tight or as loose as you want. Want a formal setup with meetings, advisors, and a board? Go for it! Want to keep things more laid-back and avoid all the bureaucracy? That works, too. The beauty of an LLC is its flexibility—run it how you see fit. You get to control the vibe, the pace, and the direction of the business. But here's where the LLC really shines: unlike a sole proprietorship, your personal assets are tucked safely out of reach. That's right—your house, car, and personal bank account? Off-limits if something goes wrong with the business. If you get hit with a lawsuit or your business stumbles into a financial pit, they can come after the LLC's assets, but your personal stuff stays locked down like a vault. It's like having all the freedom of a sole proprietorship with the legal protection of a full-blown corporation—but without all the headache of excessive paperwork, formalities, and insane fees. And let's be honest, who wants to spend more time doing paperwork than building their empire? Not you.

With an LLC, you get the best of both worlds: the protection you need to sleep at night, and the simplicity to keep hustling during the day. It's no wonder the LLC is the go-to move for serious business owners who want to play the game smarter, not harder. In other words, the LLC lets you have your cake, eat it too, and keep your wallet safe from the legal crumbs. Now that's a sweet deal!

Corporation

Now, a corporation is basically the ultimate power move in business. It's a group of people coming together to create something big, but with one goal in mind—minimizing personal risk and keeping their own assets safe. It's like forming an exclusive club where everyone's in it to win, but nobody's willing to put their personal fortunes on the line. The whole point is to separate your personal wealth from the business, so if anything goes wrong, your private assets are shielded. This isn't just a casual gathering—it's all about structure.

To form a corporation, you need a board of individuals, and not just anyone can fill these roles. You need a President to steer the ship, a Treasurer to handle the money, and a Secretary to keep everything documented (because in the world of corporations, if it's not written down, it didn't happen). These board members have to meet regularly to discuss how the business is being run, and they've got to document every decision they make.

The beauty of a corporation is that as long as everyone follows the rules and treats the business like its own separate entity, the owners, shareholders, and equity partners are safe from personal liability. If things go south—whether it's a lawsuit, a regulator, or a messy consumer issue—the most anyone can touch is the corporation's assets. Your personal house, car, and savings? Totally off-limits. It's like having a business shield that protects what's yours. But—and this is a big but—if you start crossing the lines between personal and business finances or fail to run the corporation like the independent entity it's supposed to be, you could be in for a world of trouble. That protection you thought you had? Gone. Suppose the court finds out you've been treating the business like an extension of your personal life. In that case, they'll "pierce the corporate veil," meaning your personal assets are now fair game to cover the company's liabilities.

So, running a corporation is like playing a high-stakes game of chess. It's got all the perks and protections you want, but only if you're strategic and follow the rules to the letter. Keep it clean, keep it separate, and you'll have that safety net. Mess up, and you could be left paying the price—literally.

Nonprofit

Alright, let's talk about nonprofits—the queens of doing good while playing by their own set of rules. A nonprofit organization (or NPO, if you want to sound official) is all about furthering a specific social cause or standing up for a shared belief. But don't let the "nonprofit" label fool you—these organizations can still generate income, accept donations, hold assets, and even make a profit. The difference is in how that money's handled and who gets to enjoy it. Unlike a sole proprietorship, LLC, or corporation, nonprofits can't just divvy up the profits among their members or board of directors. They're in it for the mission, not for the money.

Now, here's where things get spicy: depending on the nonprofit's purpose, donors might get the added bonus of tax deductions, which makes giving feel even better. But just because a nonprofit can make money doesn't mean it's a free-for-all. The big perk? Personal liability is limited to the nonprofit's assets—as long as everyone running the show (officers, directors, decision-makers) is following the rules to a T. Step out of line, though, and you're in trouble. If a lawsuit comes knocking and it turns out the folks in charge have been running things carelessly, their personal assets can be dragged into the mess. That's right, your house, your car, your savings—all up for grabs if you're not careful.

Now, let's get real for a second. Being a sole proprietor? It's like walking into the business world with no helmet, no game plan, and definitely no backup. You're on your own, baby! Your business assets are your personal assets. No separation, no protection. Even if you've got an EIN, you're still playing with fire. But that's where the magic of a limited liability company (LLC) comes in. When you structure your business as an LLC—which, by the way, is what I *always* recommend for my clients—you're wrapping yourself in a shield of protection. Your personal assets, your money, your retirement savings—they all stay safely behind that wall. If something goes wrong in your business, it stays in the business. Legal issues won't creep into your personal life, and you can sleep soundly, knowing your finances are safe and sound. So whether you're running a for-profit business or a nonprofit organization, it's all about structure, strategy, and having the right protections in place because no one wants to risk their personal assets when they're out here trying to change the world—or make some money.

But let's get one thing straight: when it comes to corporations, we're playing in the big leagues, and that means it's time to suit up! I often see my clients eyeing the corporate structure, thinking it's the golden ticket to success, especially regarding nonprofits. But here's the reality check: if you're diving into the corporate world, particularly with a nonprofit, you better be ready to get formal. It's a whole different ballgame compared to setting up a sole proprietorship or an LLC, where you can keep it casual and laid-back. In the corporate realm, you've got a board of directors calling the shots, and that means you need bylaws—yes, actual rules to keep everyone in line. No one wants a free-for-all when serious decisions are on the table!

If your dream involves landing funding from angel investors, hedge funds, or venture capitalists, creating a solid corporate structure is non-negotiable. This setup not only impresses potential investors but also gives you the flexibility to attract different shareholding interests and equitable investments in your company.

So, if you're aiming for that corporate crown, prepare to bring I-game. It's all about structure, strategy, and a little bit of sass to keep things exciting! But how do these business structures impact liabilities and assets? Let's examine it really quickly! In a sole proprietorship, you've got zero protection—none, zip, nada! If a lawsuit arises, the litigator, regulator, or plaintiff can go after everything you own. We're talking about your personal property, financial accounts, IRAs, savings accounts, that family savings fund for emergencies, and yes, even your Christmas fund if you still believe in those! Got some equity in your business? That's up for grabs, too. And don't even think about your cherished shoe or bag collection being safe! With no protection, anything you own can be seized as a result of a judgment against your business.

Now, flip the script! When you create a limited liability company (LLC) or a corporation, you gain a layer of protection—thank you very much! As long as you respect the regulators and separate your business operations from your personal life, you're in a much safer spot.

An even smarter strategy to secure your wealth-building legacy as a business owner is to separate your business assets, like trademarks and copyrights. Consider creating separate holding companies for those assets, and we'll get into patents and interests in other people's companies later. And remember, litigating lawyers and law firms are business owners, too. They're only after cases where they can snag a judgment and make some serious cash to compensate all interested parties. If the person causing the problem also holds the bag, you're putting your assets at serious risk. But if you separate your business assets from your business interests, you effectively remove the bag from the equation. So, keep your wealth-building legacy safe and sound by playing it smart with your business structure!

KEY FACTORS TO CONSIDER WHEN CHOOSING A BUSINESS STRUCTURE

Entrepreneurship comes in many flavors! Some folks start a side hustle just to make ends meet, while others are out there playing in the big leagues, backed by venture capital and selling equity in their businesses—think of those Shark Tank participants. But what about the everyday individual who isn't looking for funding from venture capitalists, hedge funds, or angel investors? These enterprising souls should focus on maximizing their earnings while minimizing potential liabilities and risks, ensuring their hard work pays off. To do this effectively, aspiring entrepreneurs need to assess the type of business they can handle while staying compliant with the rules and regulations. It's not just about dreaming big; it's about making informed decisions that set you up for long-term success. This means finding the simplest and most efficient way to finance personal wants, needs, and living expenses without exposing yourself to unnecessary legal liabilities. Too often, people dive into entrepreneurship without realizing that failing to formalize their finances can lead to serious consequences down the line.

A vital part of this strategy is ensuring a clear separation between personal and business assets. This means maintaining a formal banking policy that protects personal wealth and prevents those assets from being at risk in the event of legal troubles related to the business. After all, your personal property should remain just that—personal! Additionally, by setting up a structured approach to your finances, you're paving the way for future growth and success. Think about it: this allows you to easily manage your day-to-day expenses and positions you for a smoother transition when it comes time to pass down business interests to family members.

You want to create a legacy that your loved ones can thrive in, not one that leaves them untangling a financial mess. So, get smart about your entrepreneurial journey, invest the time to formalize your business operations, and protect what matters most while you're at it! But always remember, enterprising entrepreneur, that you are not your business entity! You have the power to create and control that entity, but it's essential to keep them separate.

If you have multiple entities and need to borrow money with inter-fund transactions, treat them as distinct, arm's-length transactions. The last thing you want is to create a situation where your finances get all mixed up. When you co-mingle your money, you put both yourself and your company at serious risk of being deemed an alter ego. And let me tell you, if you're labeled as an alter ego to your business (or vice versa), you lose the ability to argue that your business is separate from you in the event of a lawsuit.

That's a slippery slope, and trust me, it's not one you want to slide down!

Protect yourself and your business by maintaining clear boundaries and keeping your finances in their respective lanes. Your future self will thank you!

LEGAL BREAKDOWN: When it comes to investor-backed entrepreneurs, potential business liabilities are no joke! Protecting your assets should be your top priority, darling! The golden rule? Keep your business and personal finances completely separate—no mixing allowed! Seriously, don't even think about it! What do I mean by that? If you're sending emails from your personal account instead of your business email, honey, you're playing with fire! And signing contracts as "you" rather than as the CEO of your fabulous business? That's just asking for trouble. You need to strut into those professional situations with confidence, clearly distinguishing your personal life from your business dealings. By keeping that barrier intact, you'll safeguard your hard-earned assets and ensure your business runs like a well-oiled machine. So, channel your inner boss and keep it separate—your future self will thank you!

Holding Company

As a business owner, one of the smartest legal moves you can make is figuring out how to separate your income-generating assets from your everyday business operations—because, let's face it, you want to keep your valuable goodies safe! Enter the holding company, your new best friend. Now, before we get into the nitty-gritty, let me break it down for you in a way that's as easy as pie. Picture a holding company as a fabulous safety net for your most prized possessions—think trademarks, intellectual property, real estate, or shares in other companies. This holding company isn't out there doing the heavy lifting; it's not making sales or providing services. No, it's busy holding and protecting your valuable assets like a pro. Meanwhile, your operating company is where the real action happens—it's the powerhouse making sales, hiring employees, and taking on all those thrilling risks.

Let's throw in a sports analogy for fun: if your business were a sports team, your operating company is the star player on the field, while your holding company is chilling on the sidelines, guarding the playbook, equipment, and all the treasures. The goal? To effectively safeguard your assets from the wild risks of running a business, it's crucial to understand the distinct roles of holding and operating companies.

Holding Company: The Asset Protector

Let's get one thing straight: a holding company is not in the business of selling products or services. Nope! It's the savvy asset holder that keeps all your important business treasures under lock and key—think intellectual property, real estate, and shares in other businesses. Picture it as the ultimate gatekeeper, fiercely guarding your assets from the wild risks of lawsuits or debts that could come from your operating company. The holding company is the quiet guardian, the unsung hero that keeps your most valuable possessions safe from the chaos of the business world. It's like the wise old sage who knows how to protect the kingdom while everyone else is out there battling it out.

Operating Company: The Dream Team

Now, let's talk about the operating company—the real MVP of your business game! This is where all the action happens, the place where the magic unfolds. Think of the operating company as the athletic powerhouse on the field, actively engaging in sales, hiring top talent, making big decisions, and, yes, taking on all those delicious risks. This is where the hustle and grind come alive! The operating company utilizes the assets owned by the holding company—like renting the trademark or leveraging that fabulous intellectual property—but here's the kicker: it doesn't actually own those assets. So, if legal trouble decides to crash the party, your precious assets remain safely shielded and protected by the holding company.

So, as you can see, the holding company serves as the smart, silent protector, keeping your assets out of harm's way. In contrast, the operating company is the energetic, risk-taking force driving your business forward. Below are some additional reasons why this separation is a game-changer:

> ➤ **Liability Protection**: Picture this: your operating company gets sued. If you haven't separated your assets into a holding company, everything—your business, your intellectual property, and even your personal assets—could be at risk. Enter the holding company, acting like a fortress around your wealth. Even if your operating company faces liability, the assets owned by the holding company remain safe and sound, completely out of reach from creditors or lawsuits.

➢ **Minimizing Risk:** Running a business is like walking a tightrope; risk is always lurking beneath. From bad partnerships to unexpected legal disputes, anything can happen. By keeping your valuable assets in a holding company, you drastically minimize your exposure. The operating company can tackle all the business risks while the holding company remains insulated. If the proverbial storm hits, your assets are protected because the holding company isn't directly involved in the day-to-day chaos.

➢ **Simplified Business Sales**: Thinking about selling your business? A holding company allows you to sell the operating company—the part that handles daily operations—without letting go of your valuable assets. This is especially crucial for businesses boasting intellectual property, real estate, or trademarks. You maintain control of these assets through the holding company while still reaping the rewards of selling the operating company.

➢ **Better Control Over Assets**: With a holding company, you gain superior control over how your assets are utilized. For instance, you can license your intellectual property to other businesses or lease real estate to your operating company. This level of control ensures that your assets are working for you, all while remaining sheltered from the everyday risks of business operations.

WHAT LEGAL CHALLENGES CAN YOU FACE WHEN STRUCTURING YOUR BUSINESS?

In my experience, the common legal challenge business owners face in their early stages is the concept that just snagging an EIN (Employer Identification Number) is the golden ticket to running a legitimate business. Spoiler alert: having an EIN is different from having a properly structured business. Many folks don't realize that a business entity needs more than just that shiny number to protect your personal assets. You've got to establish a formal structure—whether that's an LLC, a corporation, or something equally sophisticated—and actually respect the rules that come with it. And let's be clear: that means having a separate EIN for each business entity.

Here's where the wheels start to come off the wagon for many entrepreneurs: they'll pile up multiple side hustles or DBAs (Doing Business As) under one business entity and naively assume that's enough. Newsflash! If you've got 10 or 12 different side hustles, each one should be treated like its own fabulous business, complete with its own bookkeeping, bank accounts, and financial records. You can't just throw everything into one pot and hope for the best! Think of each of your businesses as a child—each one deserves individual care and attention. They need separate EINs, dedicated bank accounts, meticulous bookkeeping, and tax filings (like separate Schedule C forms). You wouldn't dream of raising 20 kids under one name, right? Your businesses are no different. Each one needs its own structure to thrive and, more importantly, to safeguard your personal assets. So, stop mixing it all together and start treating your ventures like the unique powerhouses they are!

Another legal challenge I've encountered, especially as a serial entrepreneur and side hustler, is the mixing of personal and business finances. I know I just covered this, but I can't stress it enough: let's make sure you don't face a lawsuit that could obliterate your financial fortress. Seriously, I'm talking to you! I get it—many entrepreneurs are tempted to fund their ventures by dipping into personal savings, taking out 401(k) loans, or raiding other personal resources. But here's the kicker: they often neglect to document these transactions properly as business decisions. Trust me, this lack of documentation can come back to bite you in the rear when you need it the most. So, let's get it together and start treating your finances like the empire they are! This lack of paperwork can lead to major headaches down the line, particularly when it comes to safeguarding your personal assets. If you don't establish the proper paperwork and agreements, the corporate veil—the legal barrier that keeps your personal assets separate from your business—can be easily "pierced."

Think of it this way: if you're operating without a safety net, you're setting yourself up for unexpected situations—or, as I like to call them, Substantial Transactional Disorders (STDs). These are the messes that arise when personal and business finances get tangled, and they can result in dire consequences, such as losing your personal savings or being held personally liable for business debts.

Also, don't treat your business like it's your alter ego! If you're borrowing money from your personal funds, you need to create a formal agreement—just like you would with any outside lender. This isn't just a mere suggestion; it's a must. I always provide my clients with handy templates for borrowing money from themselves, ensuring they can repay the loan in a way that's legally sound and keeps their personal finances secure. Think of it as setting the boundaries that keep your financial worlds from colliding so you don't end up in a messy situation when it comes time to pay the piper.

Another crucial challenge is understanding the rules and regulations that govern your business. It's not enough to start a venture simply because it feels right or because you're passionate about it—although passion is certainly important! Business is a game, and every game comes with its own set of rules, regulations, and regulators ready to throw a flag on the play if you step out of bounds. If you ignore these rules, you could find yourself facing fines, penalties, or even being shut down faster than you can say, "entrepreneurial nightmare." So, take the time to thoroughly understand the legal landscape surrounding your business. Educate yourself on compliance issues, local laws, and industry standards. Make sure you're not just playing the game but playing it smart. After all, protecting your business is crucial for securing your wealth-building legacy and ensuring your entrepreneurial dreams don't turn into a legal horror story!

One thing I know for sure to help eliminate a whole heap of challenges is that the IRS makes it pretty simple: if you're providing a service or selling a product and you're raking in the cash, congratulations—you're officially in business! Whether you're consulting, selling a book, or offering any paid service, the IRS has you marked as a business owner. But here's the million-dollar question: how are you going to treat that business? Are you going to embrace it like a legitimate business entity, or are you just going to treat it like a side hustle to scrape together enough cash to cover your rent or mortgage? Trust me, there's a huge difference between being a sole proprietor, a gig worker, or running a fully structured business with real legal protections in place.

When you decide to engage in business, the law doesn't just take a backseat. Whether you like it or not, it comes along for the ride. And let me tell you, the law is a jealous mistress; ignore it, and you'll soon find yourself in hot water. You've got to grasp the legal rules that apply to your business because if you don't, the law will come back to haunt you—snatching away your income, your assets, and possibly more. Just look at the PPP loans for a recent example! We saw plenty of folks who didn't bother to follow the rules get turned into major cautionary tales by the IRS. When you think you can defraud a bank or bend the rules, you're opening the door to serious consequences—think criminal charges, hefty fines, and sometimes even worse. That's why it's crucial to stay on the right side of the law, familiarize yourself with the regulations that apply to your business, and protect yourself from becoming the next horror story.

So, if you're ready to create your wealth-building legacy through entrepreneurship without the legacy challenges, it's time to transform that gig or side hustle into a bona fide business! Sure, being a gig worker is all well and good, but if you want to elevate your game, you need to establish a proper business entity. Whether it's an LLC, a corporation, or even a nonprofit, it all depends on your goals and the nature of your work. And let's be real: don't get swept up in the hype of incorporating in trendy spots like Delaware or Nevada unless you're setting up a holding company.

If your business is operating in a specific state—whether you're consulting, selling real estate, or offering services—you need to register your business there. No shortcuts here! And it's always a smart move to get a registered agent. This little gem can cost as low as $25 a year, and trust me, it's essential for handling your legal documents. It keeps your operation looking professional and protects your privacy.

As your business grows, you can reassess your needs and lawyer up when it's time to level up—whether that means snagging a physical location or seeking out business credit. But in the early stages of building your wealth through entrepreneurship, you need to nail down the essentials like a boss:

- ➢ **Create a business entity:** Don't just wing it—make it official!
- ➢ **Get an EIN number:** This little gem is your ticket to legitimacy.
- ➢ **Open a separate business bank account:** Mix your personal and business finances? No thanks! Keep it clean and clear.
- ➢ **Draft an operating agreement:** Even if it's just for yourself, this document is crucial. Outline the key business details, including a succession plan in case anything happens to you. That way, your family and business partners will know exactly what to do when life throws a curveball.

And if you're working with partners, a partnership agreement is non-negotiable. Seriously, put it in writing! Protect your business, your brand, and your bank account. This paperwork is your shield, ensuring your business runs smoothly even in tough situations like illness or death. Don't leave anything to chance—get it all sorted out! And for all you dreamers thinking your business needs a trademark on day one, let me set the record straight: not every business needs a trademark right from the get-go. It all depends on whether you're building a brand or just operating under a name.

For example, a lot of law firms and service-based businesses roll with names like "Moore Legal Services," and guess what? They don't necessarily need trademark protection. However, if you're aiming to create a business that evolves into a distinct brand—think General Mills or Nike—then trademarks are your best friend. If you're thinking long-term and want to protect your brand like a boss, trademarking should definitely be on your radar early on. Before you dive into investing time and money into a name, head over to uspto.gov (the U.S. Patent and Trademark Office) to check if someone else has already bankrolled it. You can't just claim a name that's already trademarked, even if you feel like it was delivered to you on a si'ver platter. I've seen too many folks say, "God told me this is my name," but trademarks don't operate on divine intervention!

If someone else already owns it, you're opening yourself up to a world of hurt—think cease-and-desist orders and the nightmare of losing your website or social media accounts. In short, registering your business name with your state is a solid first step to establishing yourself locally. But if you want to protect your brand on a national level and build a wealth-building legacy, you need to be proactive. Secure that trademark! It's your ticket to keeping your brand safe, ensuring your name is truly yours, and preventing others from riding on your coattails.

As you can see, formalizing your business is not just a box to check; it's a critical step in building a solid foundation for your entrepreneurial journey. By establishing a legal business entity, obtaining an EIN, and maintaining separate financial accounts, you protect your personal assets from the unpredictable nature of running a business. Proper documentation, like operating and partnership agreements, acts as your shield, ensuring smooth operations even during challenging times. And let's not forget the importance of trademarks. While not every business needs one right away, securing a trademark is essential if you're serious about building a brand. It safeguards your hard-earned reputation and prevents others from capitalizing on your efforts.

Ultimately, formalizing your business sets you up for success. It helps you navigate the complexities of the legal landscape, shields your assets from liability, and positions you to grow and scale without the constant fear of legal repercussions. By taking these essential steps, you're not just protecting your business but embracing your legacy, wealth, and the financial fortress you're building. So, take the plunge, put the necessary structures in place, and watch your wealth-building legacy flourish!

SMART LEGAL MOVES REFLECTION

What's your next smart legal move to protect your wealth-building legacy? How do you define legally formalizing a business, and what steps have you taken or planned to take to ensure your business is legally recognized?

_____
_____
_____
_____
_____
_____

How do you plan to protect your business from potential legal issues that could arise in the future, and what strategies will you implement to ensure compliance?

_____
_____
_____
_____
_____
_____

Legal Move #2:
Identify & Protect Your
Intellectual Property

*Your knowledge is currency—don't let someone else cash
flow what you know without a licensing agreement.*
– Toni Moore

When it comes to protecting your brand, there is no one-size-fits-all approach to brand protection. I had a client who built a significant brand around a nonprofit, yet she never registered it before her untimely passing. Now, someone else has filed for ownership of that same brand, and they're facing an expensive legal battle to reclaim it. Although they have a priority claim, the process is proving to be costly and time-consuming. If they had filed for that trademark earlier, they wouldn't be in this predicament.

Now, let me share a personal experience. I once pitched an idea for a book and a program to a client, leading to the concept of "Divorce Like a Boss." At the time, I thought, "Let me use 'Trademark Like a Boss' to teach as an introductory class on trademarks. I didn't think of securing the brand with a trademark since I'm always using the phrase 'Like a Boss.' However, before I could consider securing the brand, another lawyer filed a trademark and DM on social media to let me know. Does that mean I can't use it? No, I can still use it because I have proof that I was using it first, but now that person has legal control over the name for her own purposes, such as podcasting, I can't create a Trademark Like a Boss podcast or book series.

This situation repeated itself with another phrase I often use: "boss up." Someone added "legally" in front of it and filed for the trademark. Again, this highlights the importance of understanding how much you value a name or brand. If it truly matters to you, if it would hurt to see someone else using it, then you need to act quickly to protect it. One of my clients made a wise decision by borrowing money to file her trademark. This turned out to be one of the smartest moves she made. Later, a bank attempted to take ownership of the name, but because she had the registration in place, she was able to stop them in their tracks. That R in the ® symbol stands for respect—it commands attention and legally protects your brand.

So, don't wait until you hit $100,000 in revenue or reach a specific milestone in your business. If a name or brand is important to you—one that you've invested in and care about—you need to file for ownership as soon as possible. The key is this: if it would pain you to see someone else using it, then trademark it. There may be ideas or names you're okay with using casually for now, but for those you genuinely want to protect and build your business around, it's time to "put a ring on it" and make it yours legally. Protecting your intellectual property isn't just smart—it's essential for safeguarding your legacy.

INTELLECTUAL PROPERTY ~ WHAT IS IT?

When it comes to Intellectual property, I always tell business owners and entrepreneurs, "Name it and claim it!" Intellectual Property (IP) is the lifeblood of your business— think of it as the crown jewels of your entrepreneurial empire. We're talking about all those brilliant inventions, catchy slogans, dazzling designs, and captivating content that your genius brain has conjured up.

IP encompasses a range of assets, including patents for innovative inventions, trademarks for your unique brand identifiers (like logos and slogans), copyrights for creative works (think books, music, and art), and trade secrets that give your business a competitive edge—recognizing what qualifies as your IP is crucial because it allows you to claim your territory in a world buzzing with creativity.

You need to understand that your unique ideas and creations have real value, and protecting them ensures that your hard work doesn't go to waste. Whether it's a groundbreaking invention that could change the world or that witty tagline that gets everyone talking, having a strong grasp of your intellectual property is key to thriving in the bustling marketplace full of copycats and wannabes.

Now, let's talk protection because you wouldn't leave your diamonds unguarded, right? Failing to protect your intellectual property is like handing out your secrets at a party and expecting everyone to keep quiet—it's not going to happen! When you don't secure your IP, you risk others cashing in on your brilliance, diluting your brand, or worse, leaving you in the dust. Imagine pouring your heart and soul into an innovative product only to find that someone else has swooped in, stolen your idea, and is now raking in the profits. You'd be furious! So, get savvy about registering those trademarks, copyrights, and patents. It's not just about playing defense; it's about boosting your business's value and making it irresistible to investors or potential buyers. Moreover, a strong IP portfolio can serve as a negotiating chip in partnerships and collaborations. Prioritizing the identification and protection of your IP isn't just smart—it's essential.

Now, I know you might be thinking, "Okay, Toni, what steps should a business take to identify and protect its IP?" Well, I'm so glad you asked! The first step is to conduct an IP review—this is your chance to get all up in your business and see what you've created, whether it's a fabulous product, a standout service, or a brand that turns heads. You want to make sure you're taking the right steps to protect it. Start by asking yourself a few questions:

> What's the name of the product, service, or brand?
> What does it do, and how does it add value to your business?
> Is it currently protected under any legal framework?

In addition, create a worksheet to document these essential elements and track how much revenue your particular name or brand is raking in. Why? Because when trademark disputes come knocking at your door, proving the distinctiveness of your brand is everything! If you can't demonstrate that your brand has value and is recognized in the market, you might as well wave goodbye to your legal standing. Knowing the monetary worth of your brand can give you a solid upper hand if anyone dares to challenge your ownership.

Once you've identified your IP, it's time to head over to uspto.gov and check if someone else is already using that name or mark. Again, not every name needs to be registered, but if it's something you've poured significant time and money into, then protecting it is a must. Think of your brand like a fabulous mansion—you wouldn't leave your doors wide open, would you? If the name represents your primary brand, you'll want to trademark it faster than you can say "intellectual property." If it's a secondary or less prominent name, you can weigh the investment and decide if it's worth your while. After all, you're building an empire, not just playing house!

Many of my clients, especially those fabulous creatives, fashionpreneurs, and beauty brand owners, often juggle multiple brand names. They have different names for their hair products, makeup lines, stores, podcasts, and even speaking gigs. Gone are the days when you could coast along with just one name for all your ventures. With so many people expanding their businesses and flaunting their creative branding, it's essential to protect the names you've monetized and refuse to lose. If you're head over heels for a name that's already raking in the cash for you, that's your cue to lock it down! A common pitfall is thinking that slapping a "™" symbol next to your brand is enough. Newsflash! That doesn't offer the robust legal protection that a registered trademark provides. To truly put some serious respect on your brand, you need to go beyond just flaunting that ™ and make sure it's officially registered. Your brand deserves nothing less than full protection!

LEGAL SIDEBAR: When it comes to protecting your intellectual property, it's all about recognizing the true value of your brand and taking proactive steps to safeguard it. Before you fall head over heels for a name or brand, make it a priority to check the USPTO website to ensure it's not already snatched up. A quick search can save you a boatload of time, cash, and a whole world of future legal headaches. Trust me, doing your homework upfront is the best way to keep your brand's reputation sparkling and drama-free!

Once you've created something valuable—whether it's a product, service, or even a framework you're proud of—the key to building and protecting your wealth-building legacy is ensuring it's legally yours. If you're out there using the name publicly and raking in revenue, that's your cue to lock it down with a registered trademark. Don't just play around with it; secure what's rightfully yours and keep those competitors at bay!

PATENTS, COPYRIGHTS, TRADEMARKS, OH MY!

Understanding the distinctions between trademarks, copyrights, and patents is essential for anyone serious about protecting their intellectual property (IP) and building a wealth-building legacy. Each form of IP serves a unique purpose: trademarks safeguard your brand identity, ensuring that your business name, logo, and slogan remain distinctly yours; copyrights protect your original creative works, such as writing, music, and art, preventing others from using them without permission; and patents secure your inventions, giving you exclusive rights to make, use, or sell your creation for a specified period.

By grasping these differences, you can confidently navigate the complex world of IP and take proactive steps to shield your innovations from infringement, ensuring that your hard work translates into lasting wealth. But since I'm the Legal Deeva, let's dive deeper into each concept so you can strut through these streets without getting manhandled!

Patents: Patents: When you hear "patent," think of the glittering crown jewels of your inventions—products or proprietary frameworks that are truly one of a kind. Patents are the guardians of creations that are new, useful, and utterly unique, much like a brilliant move on a chessboard that leaves your opponent scrambling. If you've dreamed up a product or process that no one else has even dared to imagine, it may just qualify for that coveted patent protection. With a patent, you're granted exclusive rights to use, sell, and license your brilliant invention for up to 20 glorious years.

Let me hit you with a quick story: there was a moment when I envisioned my fabulous Boss Up Bag, complete with all the bells and whistles—expandability, wheels, and a sleek design that would make anyone "love it." But before I could unleash my masterpiece, I did my homework and checked the patent database to ensure no one else had laid claim to those features. Just like in chess, where each move requires strategy and foresight, securing a patent requires careful planning and research. Trust me, that's a crucial step for anyone looking to develop a product. A patent isn't just a piece of paper; it's your "get out of jail free" card to protect and monetize your innovation! In the game of entrepreneurship, a well-timed patent can be your checkmate!

Trademarks: Think of a trademark as your brand's personal flair—like the shiny crown on a chess king that screams, "This is mine!" It's the name of your product, service, or brand that declares ownership loud and proud. When you hear names like Fashion Nova, Maybelline, or Netflix, you immediately recognize who's calling the shots. Trademarks give your brand its unique identity, helping it stand out in a sea of competitors. If you've got a killer brand name that's ready to strut its stuff in the marketplace, it's worth investing in a trademark to give it the royal treatment.

Now, not every business needs a trademark, but if you're aiming to build a brand that people instantly recognize and associate with your fabulous offerings, it's time to claim that territory and protect it. Just like in chess, where each piece has its role and protection is crucial for success, having a trademark fortifies your brand against potential threats. If your brand isn't backed by a formal business structure, it's like leaving your king exposed on the board—vulnerable to litigation and ready to be taken out by the competition. Securing your trademark not only boosts your brand's visibility but also shields it from legal risks, making it more resilient as you navigate the entrepreneurial battlefield. So, don't just play the game—own it!

Copyrights: I like to say, "C is for creative works," and let me tell you, copyright is the crown jewel of protecting everything you've poured your heart into—whether it's a book, music, choreography, artwork, or even a course. It's all about taking that spark of creativity and locking it down in a tangible form. Copyright gives you the legal power to reproduce, distribute, and safeguard those masterpieces you've crafted. Now, if you're teaming up with others, you better make sure your agreement is as clear as a chess strategy—who owns the copyright? Is it you, the genius behind the creation, or the business that commissioned it? Nail down that clarity to dodge any disputes down the line and keep your creative reign intact.

And let's squash that old-school myth of the "poor man's copyright"—you know, the one where folks mail themselves a copy of their work like it's some kind of secret weapon. That's so outdated it belongs in the medieval times! Your creativity is your key to wealth, so treat it like the treasure it is by registering your copyright properly. Just like in chess, where every piece has its role and protecting your queen is crucial, safeguarding your creative works ensures that no one can step in and claim your brilliance as their own. Play smart, protect your assets, and watch your creative empire flourish!

SMART LEGAL MOVE

Always do your homework and conduct a search on uspto.gov before you start using or registering any name, product, or creative work. This step is crucial for ensuring you're not stepping on someone else's intellectual property toes. Don't let a preventable infringement issue come back to bite you!

By understanding the distinct roles of trademarks, copyrights, and patents, you'll be equipped to protect your business and build your legacy. Think of it as putting legal armor around what makes your business valuable—whether it's your brand name, creativity, or innovative products. This savvy approach helps ensure that what's rightfully yours stays safe from those who might try to snatch it away!

IP & WORK FOR HIRE

When it comes to intellectual property, everything is negotiable. If you don't have a contractual agreement that clearly outlines creative rights and copyright ownership, the default rule is that whoever creates it owns it. That's right—if you're hiring someone to whip up that brilliant design or write that catchy jingle, you better get those terms in writing before the creative juices start flowing! Without this clarity, you could find yourself in a precarious situation that is tricky to resolve.

You see, when companies or individuals bring creatives on board—be it for a record deal, a bestselling book, or a standout design—they ensure the contract explicitly states that any work created under that agreement will belong to them. The catch? The creative often ends up categorized as an independent contractor rather than a co-owner of the venture. So, if you're the one doing the hiring, it's crucial to negotiate ownership rights upfront. For instance, if you're commissioning illustrations for a children's book, the illustrator might agree to let you use their work exclusively for your project. But here's the kicker: if they retain ownership of the original artwork, you're left as a mere licensee, not the full owner of the IP. This is where things can get complicated. You might think you're set to launch your fabulous new project, only to realize you don't have the rights to fully exploit or sell the creative work you thought was yours. That's why I always say: CYA—Cover Your Assets—with clear, detailed contracts! Everything is negotiable until it isn't, and the best time to hammer out those IP ownership and usage rights is before the work is created before misunderstandings bloom, and definitely, before any legal drama unfolds. Don't let the excitement of the creative process blind you to the essential details—getting these agreements in writing protects your assets and the legacy you're building. By taking the time to establish these terms, you set yourself up for a smoother journey toward success, allowing you to focus on what you do best: creating!

LEGAL SIDEBAR:

- Work for Hire: In the realm of intellectual property (IP) law, this term refers to a scenario where the employer or the person commissioning the work gets to strut around with the copyright—if there's a clear agreement that spells it out, of course. If that agreement is missing, guess what? The creator retains ownership. So, don't forget to dot those i's and cross those t's!
- Independent Contractor: This is the fabulous individual you hire to tackle a specific task—be it whipping up a stunning design or penning a bestseller. But beware! Unless you've got a contract that says otherwise, this creative genius keeps the rights to their masterpiece.
- Joint Venture Partner: Think of this as the ultimate collaboration! When two or more parties join forces to share ownership and control over a project or creative work, that's a joint venture partnership. It's

all about teamwork and mutual benefits—just make sure everyone knows their role and rights!

SMART LEGAL MOVE

Always pack your contracts with clear language about who owns the copyright—whether it's a full transfer of ownership or just a limited license. Nail down these terms from the get-go to safeguard your business interests and dodge any future drama. Trust me, being proactive now will save you from headaches later!

Alright, let's get real for a second. If you are already knee-deep in a business relationship without a contract, don't throw in the towel just yet—there's still hope! The golden rule is to negotiate your intellectual property rights before delivering your masterpiece. This is your golden opportunity to lay claim to the value of your creativity, time, and effort, ensuring that they translate into something that boosts your wealth-building legacy. But if you're reading this and having a mini-panic attack because you skipped that crucial step, take a page out of Donald Trump's playbook—yes, the Donald—who famously renegotiated his post-nuptial agreements more times than anyone can count. So, what should you do? First off, don't just sit there twiddling your thumbs like you're waiting for a bus! Get proactive! Pick up that phone or shoot over an email and reach out to the other party to negotiate your terms. Here's how to handle it like a boss:

> ➤ **Prepare Your Case**: Before you meet, gather all the relevant information about your contributions.

Outline your work and the value it brings to the table. Remember, confidence is key!

➤ **Set Up a Meeting**: Don't be shy! Schedule a sit-down where you can both discuss the specifics. This shows that you're serious and professional.

➤ **Be Clear About Your Goals**: During the conversation, make it clear what you want. Are you looking for a full transfer of ownership? A limited license? Spell it out, darling!

➤ **Use Written Agreements**: Once you reach an understanding, make sure everything is documented. A verbal agreement is nice, but it's as good as a handshake with a ghost if it's not in writing.

➤ **Stay Professional**: Even if the conversation gets a little heated (and let's be real, it might), keep your cool. You want to maintain a professional relationship, especially if you're continuing to work together.

And let's be clear: your equitable interest isn't just some legal jargon; it represents cold, hard cash and the value of your hard work contributing to your wealth-building legacy. Every time you create something valuable—be it a product, service, or killer content—you're investing in your future. So, don't let that investment go unprotected! By negotiating your rights now, you're securing the future returns of your work, just like you would with any other smart business move. Remember, every creator deserves compensation for their brilliance, so get out there and ensure your IP is locked down tighter than Fort Knox!

USING INTELLECTUAL PROPERTY TO SECURE A COMPETITIVE ADVANTAGES

One of the key advantages of securing intellectual property (IP) in business is understanding its immense power as a strategic asset. When evaluating a company—whether for acquisition or assessing overall value—one of the first indicators we look for is the presence of registered IP. This isn't about common law trademarks or informal copyrights; we're talking about registered assets that come with documented proof of ownership. These registrations provide a solid foundation for assessing the business's brand equity. For instance, I always advise my clients to meticulously track the first use of their trademark, how it's being used, and the revenue generated annually from it. This practice is essential for due diligence and plays a critical role in determining the true value of the IP. Unfortunately, many business owners undervalue their brand equity because they see their IP as just a simple certificate rather than the invaluable asset it truly represents.

SHIFTING YOUR MINDSET: FROM CERTIFICATE TO CURRENCY

When you shift your mindset from viewing your IP as just a fancy piece of paper to seeing it as currency, you unlock the true potential of your creativity. Intellectual property isn't just a certificate; it's a powerful asset that can open doors to a whole new world of opportunities. Think about it: you can use your IP as collateral in financial dealings or as a serious bargaining chip in joint ventures and partnerships. It's like having a golden ticket in your back pocket!

Let's take a page from The Profit, where Marcus Lemonis swoops in like a hawk. He negotiated ownership interest in a company's trademark, and guess what? The business owner had no clue about the goldmine they were sitting on. In a shocking twist, they gave away a whopping 70% ownership to Lemonis! Talk about a bad deal! He gained major control over the business while the original owner was left holding just a tiny piece of the pie—literally a fraction of the profits they could have enjoyed.

The lesson here is crystal clear: treat your IP as a strategic asset from the get-go. Don't just sit back and hope for the best; be proactive in protecting and leveraging it. By doing so, you can secure a competitive advantage that doesn't just boost your business growth but adds real financial value to your empire. So, ladies and gentlemen, don't underestimate your intellectual property. It's not just a certificate; it's your ticket to the big leagues!

Key Takeaways
- Assess the Value: Regularly evaluate your IP's contribution to your business, including how it generates revenue and enhances brand recognition.
- Document Everything: Keep detailed records of IP usage and first use dates, which can help protect your rights and negotiate future deals.
- Leverage Your IP: Your IP can be a powerful asset in negotiations, partnerships, and securing financing.

By embracing these practices, you protect your business and position it for greater success in the marketplace. Intellectual property is not just a legal formality; it's a cornerstone of your business strategy and wealth-building legacy.

GAINING OWNERSHIP IN SOMEONE'S TRADEMARK

You can negotiate ownership of a trademark just like you would with real estate or brand equity in a business. Before we dive into trademarks, how many of you have heard the term "brand equity" or know what it means? I can see some of you raising your eyebrows, so let me break it down for you first, and then we'll reconvene on how to gain ownership. Deal? Brand equity is like an asset—just as valuable as real estate or the worth of a company. The more you use and promote your brand, the more recognition it gains and the more valuable it becomes. Think of it as building equity over time. When you start leveraging that brand through licensing agreements, partnerships, or even franchising, you're treating it like a real business asset. For instance, as your brand begins generating significant income, people will start to take notice. Some may want to buy into it or get a piece of it. That's where brand equity comes into play. It's akin to evaluating a company—when determining its value, we look at receivables, customer base, assets, and revenue. The same applies to brand equity, whether it's tied to a trademark, a book, or any piece of intellectual property.

Imagine a publishing company collaborating with an influencer to create a book, then expanding that brand with workbooks, courses, and other related products. Each of those new offerings adds to the brand's equity because they generate more revenue and reach a wider audience. Essentially, the more money the brand generates, the higher its value becomes, which means others may want to leverage it for their own purposes. It's all about valuation—the more you build up the brand, the more equity it holds. This reminds me of my time as a divorce attorney. During separations, we'd always analyze equitable distribution; from the start of the marriage to the end, we'd assess how much value had accumulated. In the same way, brand equity is the accumulation of value over time as you invest in and grow your brand. So, overall, brand equity is the key to transforming your brand into a powerful asset that can drive financial success and open doors for future opportunities— got it! Great.

So, let's get to the topic at hand: a trademark is a piece of intellectual property that holds value akin to any other asset. Whether through collateral agreements, joint ventures, or partnership deals, you can gain an interest in a trademark. Consider how companies often leverage their trademarks similarly to how musicians capitalize on their music rights. Take Hypnosis Records, for example. They've acquired the rights to hit songs, transforming them into valuable assets and creating billion-dollar equity deals. You can adopt a similar approach with your trademark by establishing a framework that tracks its usage, revenue generation, licensing agreements, and overall brand equity.

To gain ownership or a stake in someone else's trademark, you'd negotiate a licensing agreement, an equity deal, or a joint venture. The essence lies in recognizing that every trademark possesses potential value and can be monetized through licensing, royalty agreements, or even used as collateral for business deals. The key is having the foresight to protect that trademark from the outset.

Many entrepreneurs overlook the legal aspects of intellectual property protection, but as you scale your business, it becomes imperative to "lawyer up" to ensure you're safeguarding and maximizing the value of your trademarks and other assets. By treating your trademark as a valuable business component, you protect your interests and enhance your potential for growth and profitability. Don't leave money on the table—make sure your trademarks are as well-defended as your other business ventures!

LEGAL CONSEQUENCES OF FAILING TO SAFEGUARD YOUR IP PROPERLY

The worst thing that can happen is one of two scenarios. First, you put your idea or creation out into the world, and someone else takes it—because ideas themselves aren't protected. This scenario can lead to the frustration of seeing someone else reap the benefits of your hard work while you're left empty-handed. Second, you entrust your intellectual property (IP) to someone without proper safeguards, and they run off with it. The reality is that without legal protections in place, you're leaving yourself vulnerable to exploitation. Let me share a real-life example: A woman I knew started a cookie business with a friend using her family's secret recipe. They were excited to launch their venture, but crucially, they didn't have an agreement in place outlining each partner's responsibilities and rights. When the partnership ended, her friend took the recipes, changed the business name, and continued selling the same cookies without her. It's a harsh lesson in why you must appreciate the legalities of business. Legal agreements don't just protect you; they also restrict others from taking what's rightfully yours.

I've encountered many situations where individuals didn't fully understand the value of their IP until it was almost too late. During her divorce, one of my clients was fortunate that her spouse didn't successfully go after her brand name. Even though she hadn't fully productized her business at that point, the potential of that brand was undeniable. I repeatedly told her how she could 10X its value, and she eventually recognized how critical it was that her spouse didn't have the resources or legal leverage to fight for ownership. Had she not taken steps to protect her IP, her ex could have easily claimed ownership of her brand, leaving her on the sidelines, watching someone else profit from her hard work and vision.

The lesson here is simple: protect your IP from the beginning. Failing to do so could result in someone else taking control of what you've worked so hard to build. Whether it's a name, a recipe, a business idea, or any form of creative output, safeguarding your intellectual property is essential for maintaining control over your legacy. It ensures that you can continue to innovate and grow without the fear of someone else capitalizing on your creativity.

PRACTICAL STEPS TO PROTECT YOUR IP

- ➢ **Draft Clear Agreements**: Always have legal agreements in place before you share your ideas or collaborate with others. This includes partnership agreements, licensing contracts, and non-disclosure agreements (NDAs). These documents clarify ownership rights and usage terms, minimizing misunderstandings.
- ➢ **Register Your IP**: Take proactive steps to register your trademarks, copyrights, or patents. While common law protections exist, registered IP

provides you with a stronger legal standing in case of disputes.

➢ **Document Everything**: Keep records of your creative process, including drafts, designs, and development stages. This documentation can serve as evidence of your ownership and the timeline of your work, which can be crucial in legal disputes.

➢ **Educate Yourself**: Familiarize yourself with the basics of intellectual property law. Understanding the different types of IPs and how they work can empower you to make informed decisions and protect your assets effectively.

➢ **Seek Legal Counsel**: As your business grows, consider consulting with an intellectual property attorney. They can provide tailored advice and strategies to safeguard your IP and navigate the complexities of IP law.

By taking these proactive measures now, you'll be better positioned to navigate the complexities of your entrepreneurial journey with confidence. Remember, protecting your intellectual property isn't just about safeguarding your current work; it's an investment in your future growth and success. But let me warn you: if you don't protect your intellectual property, it can be taken or stolen. That's why I always say, "trademark it or lose it." In fact, I've created an e-book and a class called Trademark It First specifically for this reason. If you fail to protect your brand and assets with the right legal tools, leave the door open for someone else to claim what you've worked so hard to create.

Here's the thing—just like many women don't want to talk about prenups, some business owners hesitate to take those essential protective legal steps. They might feel that doing so is too aggressive or worry that it might alienate potential partners or clients. However, there comes a time when you can't afford to be demure in business. It's crucial to recognize that protecting your intellectual property is not just a defensive move; it's a strategic one. Sometimes, you've got to level up and demand more: more protection, more legal safeguards, more equity, and stronger boundaries. This is about asserting your value and ensuring that your hard work is recognized and rewarded.

Remember, running a business is like playing a game. As a former basketball player, I can tell you it's not just about showing up and dribbling—you need a solid game plan. You must know who your key players are, who's motivating you, who's watching, and how you're going to execute your strategy.

Every move matter, and you need to appreciate the consequences of each decision, just like in chess. And let's be honest: if you're a woman in business, remember that God made you a queen. You're not just one-dimensional; you can move in multiple directions. But to do so effectively, you've got to know your value and claim your queendom.

Don't let anyone treat you like a pawn on the board. You need to position yourself powerfully, empower yourself, and continually invest in your growth—whether through reading, taking courses, or making bold moves like I did when I took out a 401k loan to fund my entrepreneurial journey. Money can't be an excuse. If we let money stop us, we excuse ourselves from reaching our full potential. You have to shift your mindset and recognize that you can be the first millionaire in your family or that you deserve prosperity as your birthright. Visualize your brand making $50,000, $100,000, or even $750,000 a year, and then set that goal and go for it. Don't wait for someone else to take the shot—own your role in this game.

PROTECTING YOUR IP INTERNATIONALLY

Every country has its own rules regarding intellectual property protection, so it's definitely not a one-size-fits-all situation. In the United States, the first step is to file your trademark in your home country. The U.S. is a fabulous hub for intellectual property protection, and once you've filed here, you can strut your stuff and take advantage of agreements like the Hague Convention, which lets you file a priority claim in over 50 other countries. But remember darling—you still need to file separately in each country where you want protection. Now, you don't have to file in every country if you're not operating globally. But if you are—especially for my fashionpreneurs and those with international business interests in places like the UK—you need to protect your IP in each of those markets. Just because you've got a trademark locked down in one country doesn't mean it's automatically safe everywhere else.

Let's talk about China for a second. China has its own IP laws, and guess what? It doesn't just roll out the red carpet for U.S. trademarks. If you want to protect your brand in China, you need to file directly there and play by their rules. So, if you're planning to go international, you need to be ready to tango with the legal requirements of each country. Filing in the U.S. is a fabulous first step, but it won't protect you globally unless you take further action in those other territories. In short, it's all about knowing your rights and making sure your business is protected wherever you decide to shine. Filing in the U.S. helps you keep infringers away, but if you're thinking globally, you've got to roll up your sleeves and get specific with each market.

Now, when it comes to trademarks, they operate a bit differently in our global economy. With trademarks, you need to think big—your brand can be used or recognized across borders, so you can't just stick to your home turf. Believe it or not, there have been major U.S. companies that lost their patents or trademarks in other countries simply because they didn't file for protection outside the U.S. It's a harsh reality!

In the business world, there's always someone lurking in the shadows, ready to snatch up your intellectual property. You've got to stay sharp, keep your eyes wide open, and take the necessary steps to protect your assets. Don't leave your hard work up for grabs—be proactive and make sure your brand is safe wherever it goes!

What about patents? Now, let me be clear—I'm not a patent attorney. Those folks usually have a science background, and there are even patent mentors out there who aren't lawyers but guide others through the patent process based on their own experience. But let me tell you, if you find yourself in a pickle in another country, there are plenty of resources to help you. I'm part of an IP lawyer fellowship with over 3,000 attorneys from around the globe, so I've got connections if my clients need international support. The real secret sauce? You need to protect your home base first— where your primary business is thriving—before you start spreading that protection to other countries where you're making money or building your fabulous brand.

For those of you strutting your stuff as global entrepreneurs or fabulous expats, you've got to be extra mindful. When you're out there building generational wealth through your intellectual property, consulting, or business ventures, registrations are your BFFs—they're essentially your receipts of ownership. We're talking about legal documents—your deeds, certificates, trademarks, and registrations—that prove what you own. Without those receipts, good luck trying to play detective for your heirs to find your assets. No one is going to hand them a map to your wealth! And don't even get me started on privacy issues. Without proper documentation, proving ownership is like trying to find a needle in a haystack. It's just like cryptocurrency—if you don't have the receipt for your wallet, it's as if your assets might as well be vapor. So, get your ducks in a row and make sure your IP is buttoned up tight!

Overall, when it comes to protecting your brand, there is no one-size-fits-all approach to brand protection. I had a client who built a significant brand around a nonprofit, yet she never registered it before her untimely passing. Now, someone else has filed for ownership of that same brand, and they're facing an expensive legal battle to reclaim it. Although they have a priority claim, the process is proving to be costly and time-consuming. If they had filed for that trademark earlier, they wouldn't be in this predicament.

Now, let me share a personal experience. I once pitched an idea for a book and a program to a client, leading to the concept of "Divorce Like a Boss." At the time, I thought, "Let me trademark 'Trademark Like a Boss' for myself." However, before I could file, someone who knew I was using it preemptively filed for it themselves. Does that mean I can't use it? No, I can still use it because I have proof that I was using it first, but now that person has legal control over the name for her own purposes, such as podcasting. This situation repeated itself with another phrase I often use: "boss up." Someone added "legally" in front of it and filed for the trademark. Again, this highlights the importance of understanding how much you value a name or brand. If it truly matters to you, if it would hurt to see someone else using it, then you need to act quickly to protect it.

One of my clients made a wise decision by borrowing money to file her trademark. This turned out to be one of the smartest moves she made. Later, a bank attempted to take ownership of the name, but because she had the registration in place, she was able to stop them in their tracks. That R in the ® symbol stands for respect—it commands attention and legally protects your brand. So, don't wait until you hit $100,000 in revenue or reach a specific milestone in your business.

If a name or brand is important to you—one that you've invested in and care about—you need to file for ownership as soon as possible. The key is this: if it would pain you to see someone else using it, then trademark it. There may be ideas or names you're okay with using casually for now, but for those you genuinely want to protect and build your business around, it's time to "put a ring on it" and make it yours legally. Protecting your intellectual property isn't just smart—it's essential for life-long currency.

SMART LEGAL MOVES REFLECTION

What proactive measures are you currently implementing to monitor potential infringements of your intellectual property, and how can you enhance these strategies to better protect your assets?

_____
_____
_____
_____
_____
_____
_____
_____
_____
_____
_____
_____
_____
_____

In what ways can you leverage your intellectual property to create additional revenue streams, such as licensing agreements or collaborations, and what steps will you take to pursue these opportunities?

_____

_____

_____

_____

_____

_____

_____

_____

How can you integrate your intellectual property strategy
into your overall business plan to ensure that you maximize
its value while minimizing risks?

_____

_____

_____

_____

_____

_____

_____

_____

Legal Move #3:
Trademark it First!

Secure your brand with legal protections to avoid public and financial battles—because once it's in the spotlight, everyone wants a piece of it. – Toni Moore

Toni, I need a trademark! Toni, when should I get a trademark? Toni, what can I trademark, and how much do you charge?" Let me tell you—over the past five years, trademarks have blown up like TikTok dances. Seriously, you can't go five minutes on Instagram or TikTok without someone—lawyers, influencers, your cousin's friend's boyfriend—trying to hustle you a trademark like it's the new "it" thing. It's gotten to the point where snagging a trademark feels as simple as getting an EIN number. But let's slow down for a second, okay? Yes, trademarks are crucial—absolutely crucial—for protecting your business, your brand, your intellectual property, and all the things that matter when you're building your empire. But here's the real tea: Do you even know what a trademark really is? Like, beyond the hype and hustle, do you understand what it's for, how to maintain it, and what it's actually protecting? This isn't some cute little box you check off and then move on like you're done. After you "pay" for your trademark, what happens next? What's your game plan with it?

Some of y'all are trademarking things that don't even need it. You're throwing money at stuff just because somebody on social media said you should, but you don't even know why. And then there's the other side of the coin—some of y'all are out here with legit brands, real businesses that desperately need trademark protection, and you're just letting them float out there vulnerable, like they don't matter. Spoiler alert: they do.

Here's the thing: not every cute idea or catchy phrase needs a trademark. I know it's tempting to throw a trademark on anything that moves because, let's face it, everyone's doing it like it's the latest fashion trend. But a trademark is not a purse you carry around to show off—it's a serious legal tool. And baby, just like with any tool, if you don't know how to use it, you're going to get hurt. A trademark is meant to protect your hard work and to guard your business from people trying to ride your coattails and swipe what's yours. But only if you're protecting the right things. So before you jump on the trademark bandwagon because it's trending on your feed, stop and think: Do I actually need this? Do I even know what a trademark does? And if you're already paying for one, don't just sit on it like it's some kind of status symbol. There's work involved! You've got to maintain it, enforce it, make sure it's serving its purpose. Otherwise, why are you even doing it?

Let's get real. Some of you are out here treating trademarks like the latest fashion accessory—cute but not essential—when, in reality, it's the armor that's going to protect your brand for the long haul. Others are naked on the battlefield, completely unprotected, while everyone else is suiting up. If you're serious about building a business that lasts, then get serious about understanding what you need and why. And if you're still confused, keep reading because we are about to have a real legal conversation about trademarks, what's worth protecting, and what's just trendy fluff.

WHAT IS A TRADEMARK?

A trademark isn't just a pretty logo or a clever slogan—it's your brand's personal bouncer, keeping the copycats and lookalikes from getting in on your hard-earned success. Imagine building a thriving business and creating an unforgettable brand, only to watch someone else snatch up your name, slap it on their stuff, and reap the benefits. Without a trademark, that's a real risk. But when you trademark your business name, logo, or even your signature catchphrase, you're doing more than slapping a stamp on it—you're locking it down. You're telling the world, "This is mine, and no one else can use it." It's about owning your space in the market and making sure you don't lose what's rightfully yours. A trademark is like putting a moat around your business, turning it into a financial fortress that no one can easily breach.

Without one, you're rolling the dice on your brand's future. You've put in the work, the late nights, and probably a few tears to build something meaningful. Don't let someone else bankroll on your success because you didn't take the steps to protect it. A trademark isn't just a nice-to-have—it's a must-have for any business that wants to play the long game, keeping your brand identity safe, your reputation secure, and your profits exactly where they belong: with you. So, before we go any further, let's break it down! When it comes to trademarks, you can't just slap a ™ on anything and call it a day. There are specific rules about what can and can't be trademarked, and knowing the difference can save you a lot of time, money, and headaches. So, here's the tea:

What *CAN* be Trademarked:

> ➤ **Business Names** – Your business name can be trademarked as long as it's distinctive and not too generic. Think of names like Nike or Apple— they're unique to those brands, so they're protected.

> ➤ **Logos** – That iconic swoosh or bitten apple? Yep, logos are a huge part of what businesses trademark because it helps customers visually recognize them instantly.

> ➤ **Slogans** – "Just Do It." "I'm Lovin' It." Memorable phrases that are closely tied to your brand can be trademarked so others can't use them.

> ➤ **Product Names** – If you have a specific product that stands out, like "iPhone" or "Big Mac," that product name can be trademarked.

> ➤ **Sounds** – Yes, sounds can be trademarked too! The NBC chimes or the MGM lion's roar are good examples of trademarked sounds. If it's a unique sound associated with your brand, you can protect it.

> ➤ **Symbols and Designs** – Custom symbols or design elements that are recognizable as part of your brand can be trademarked.

➢ **Colors (in some cases)** – If a color is distinctively associated with your brand and not commonly used in your industry, you can trademark it. For example, Tiffany & Co. trademarked that iconic Robin's egg blue.

➢ **Taglines and Catchphrases** – Those catchy one-liners that represent your brand, like "Have It Your Way" or "Think Different," can be trademarked too.

What *CAN NOT* be Trademarked:

➢ **Generic Terms** – You can't trademark a term that's too common in your industry. For example, trying to trademark the word "pizza" for a pizza place? Not happening. It's way too generic.

➢ **Descriptive Words** – If your business name or logo simply describes what you sell, like "Fresh Flowers" for a florist, it's not unique enough to trademark. You need to be more creative!

➢ **Government Symbols** – You can't trademark flags, government seals, or anything associated with government entities. Sorry, the U.S. flag or the presidential seal is off-limits.

➢ **Geographical or Landmark Names** – that could be misleading (like trying to trademark "I Love New York" when you're not even in the state) or names tied to famous landmarks (think "London Bridges" or "Eiffel Tower").

➢ **Common Phrases or Idioms** – If it's something that's commonly used in everyday language, like "Have a Nice Day" or "Good Morning," you can't claim it for your own.

- ➤ **Functional Features** – Anything that's purely functional, like the shape of a product that serves a practical purpose (e.g., the shape of a bottle that makes it easier to hold) cannot be trademarked. Trademarks are for branding, not functionality.
- ➤ **Deceptive Marks** – You can't trademark something that would mislead consumers. For example, you can't trademark "Healthy Snacks" if your product is actually loaded with sugar.
- ➤ **An Existing Trademark** – You can't trademark something that's just a knockoff of an existing trademark. Trademarks protect names, phonetic sounds, trade dress (like that signature Tiffany blue or specific color schemes like the AKA sorority's colors), and even sounds (think of the iconic Netflix intro sound—it's a registered trademark, baby!).
- ➤ **Surnames (in some cases)** – Common last names usually can't be trademarked unless they have gained a secondary meaning, like McDonald's. If you're trying to trademark "Smith Plumbing," that's probably too common to get approved.
- ➤ **Offensive or Scandalous Material** – Anything that could be deemed offensive, immoral, or scandalous will be shot down. The trademark office isn't having it.

Overall, a trademark protects anything that distinguishes your brand from others and helps your customers recognize you—whether that's a name, logo, slogan, or even a sound. But if it's too generic, descriptive, or functional, you're out of luck. Just remember, trademarks are all about making your business stand out, so the more unique, the better!

Alright, so now that you know what to trademark and what not to, you're ready to level up and lock down that trademark. So next, let's talk about how you actually get it and how long it will take because, spoiler alert—it's not an instant gratification process. Trademarking can happen at both the state and national levels, but if you're trying to play big, you must focus on national protection. That's where I roll. You might need state-level coverage, too, but even then, the state will want to know if you've got your national trademark game on point.

So, how do you get started? You've got two options: you can either hire a lawyer to handle the heavy lifting or use one of those online service providers that claim to make it "easy." But no matter which route you take, the process involves several steps—so don't think you're just filling out a form and getting your shiny new certificate in the mail next week. Here's a few of those steps because, as your legal deeva, I can't let you roll into this unprotected:

➢ **Name Your Trademark** ~ First things first, what exactly are you trademarking? Is it your brand name, product name, slogan, or logo? Get clear on that. This is the foundation, so, no pressure—but you better pick something that's unique and memorable!

➢ **Do Your Homework (AKA Search for Existing Trademarks)** ~ Before you start throwing money around, make sure your trademark isn't already taken. Head to the USPTO's Trademark Electronic

Search System (TESS) and do a quick search to see if your brilliant idea is already out there. If it is, back to the drawing board, Babe. You need something fresh.

➢ **Choose Your Class (45 Categories, Pick Your Lane(s))** ~ There are 45 different trademark classes that cover all kinds of businesses. And let me tell you, these categories cover everything—from podcasting to running an online store to Software as a Service (SaaS). Whatever you're up to with your brand, trust me, there's a category for it. Feeling overwhelmed by all those options? Don't stress— I've got you covered. In my Trademark It First Guidebook, I break down all 45 categories so you can easily figure out exactly where your brand fits. No guessing games, just straight-up clarity!

➢ **File Your Application with the USPTO** ~ Now it's game time! Head to the United States Patent and Trademark Office (USPTO) website and start filling out the application. You'll need to provide:
  o Your name and business info
  o A description of your trademark
  o The category (class) your trademark falls under
  o A sample of how your trademark is used (like on packaging, websites, etc.)
  o A filing fee for each class you want to trademark (yes, it costs $$$, but it's worth it).

➢ **Wait for the USPTO Examiner's Review** ~ Here comes the waiting game. After submitting, a USPTO examiner will review your application to ensure everything's in order. This could take a few months, so don't be blowing up their phone. If they find any issues, they'll let you know, and you'll have the chance to respond and make adjustments.

➤ **Publication for Opposition** ~ If your application passes the initial review, it'll be published in the Official Gazette (sounds fancy, right?). If no one raises a fuss if they think you're stepping on their territory within 30 days, then congratulations! Your trademark gets the green light for approval.

  o This is the step that many either fail or have to really identify the uniqueness of your filing. A common issue with trademarks is that some terms or phrases may be overused, making them harder to protect. For example, I use the phrase "Like a Boss" all the time, but it's widely used, so trademarking that alone would be difficult. However, if you add a unique twist to it—like I did with other variations of the phrase—you may still be able to trademark it. So, the key is ensuring that what you're trademarking is distinct and filing the paperwork as early as possible to avoid complications down the line.

➤ **Approval and Registration** ~ If everything goes smoothly, you'll finally get that official trademark registration from the USPTO. Cue the confetti because your brand is now protected! Pop that champagne, but don't forget—trademarks aren't set-it-and-forget-it. You'll need to maintain it with periodic filings, or it could get canceled.

> ➢ **Maintain Your Trademark** ~ Your trademark needs to be renewed periodically. Your trademark is typically valid for five to six years. Around the fifth year, the USPTO will hit you up for a maintenance filing to make sure you're still rocking that trademark in your business. They'll want to verify your usage through your marketing and advertising efforts. Basically, you need to prove that your trademark is still actively in play within your trade, business, or services. After that initial maintenance filing, you'll need to check in every 10 years to keep your trademark alive and kicking.

PROTECTING YOUR TRADEMARK IS A SMART LEGAL MOVE

Protecting your trademark isn't just a smart legal move; it's an absolute power play in the dog-eat-dog world of business. Picture this: you've invested blood, sweat, and endless cups of coffee into building a brand that truly embodies your vision and passion. You're finally hitting your stride, and when you think you're cruising, someone else comes along, takes your hard work, and serves it up as their own. Not on my watch! Look, your brand is your baby, and you wouldn't let just anyone waltz in and mess with it, right?

With trademark protection, you can confidently strut your stuff, knowing that your identity is safeguarded. It's like wearing a fabulous outfit that turns heads everywhere you go—your brand deserves that kind of recognition! When customers see your trademark, they'll instantly know it's you, and there will be no mistaking it. And we all know how important brand recognition is in a world flooded with options; you want to be the one that stands out in a sea of sameness.

But wait, there's more! Trademarking isn't just about protection; it's about boosting your business's value. Think of it as adding a designer handbag to your outfit—it elevates your entire presence! A solid trademark can transform your brand into a valuable asset, making it super appealing if you ever want to sell or expand your operations. Plus, the peace of mind that comes with knowing you're legally covered allows you to unleash your creativity without fear.

Also, you should know that once you have your trademark, there are several ways to monitor and enforce your trademark rights. And let me tell you, this is no time to kick back and relax! Sure, some companies specialize in IP monitoring using the latest AI wizardry, and as a lawyer, I help my clients with this, too. But here's the kicker—you can't just set it and forget it. It would help if you had someone on your team actively watching over your brand like a hawk, ready to swoop in at the first sign of trouble.

One of the simplest and most cost-effective ways to monitor your brand is by setting up Google Alerts. It's like having a personal assistant without the coffee runs! Just set up alerts for your brand name, and voila—you'll get notifications whenever it pops up online. You could also have someone on your team—like an intern, a savvy friend, or even one of your kids—diligently scrolling through social media to sniff out any unauthorized uses of your brand. And let's be real: when you're lounging on the couch, Netflixing your latest binge, take a few minutes to do a quick IP search. It's an easy way to ensure no one infringes on your rights while trying to enjoy your guilty pleasure!

Another way to stay on top of things is to add your brand to the USPTO.gov watch list once it's registered. This nifty feature helps you keep tabs on potential infringements so you can act swiftly if anything pops up! If you're juggling multiple brands (and let's be real, who isn't these days?), especially more than 10, it's wise to hire a brand monitoring company to help you manage the chaos. Because, darling, if you're not careful, things can slip through the cracks faster than you can say "trademark infringement." You don't want to find out someone's been using your brand without your knowledge—especially not after they've grown big enough to make a dent in your market.

Here's the thing: registering your trademark is just the first step in this wild adventure. As the business owner, the law requires you to actively protect your brand and ensure its value isn't diminished. You can't just rely on the registration; you need to be the vigilant guardian of your intellectual property, monitoring it like a hawk to prevent unauthorized use.

TRADEMARK: CAN MULTIPLE PARTNERS OWN IT?

When a business has multiple partners, the question of trademark ownership can get a little dicey. Who owns the trademark? Should it be trademarked under all the partners? Well, here's the deal: there's no one-size-fits-all answer when it comes to brand ownership in a partnership. However, the smartest move is to think like an asset-protecting lawyer and prepare for the worst-case scenario—like, you know, if the partnership takes a nosedive and emotions run high. If you haven't laid down the law with clear agreements from the get-go, things can get messy faster than a spilled drink at a party.

It's kind of like a prenup for your business—what I like to call a "business nuptial agreement." This little gem outlines who owns what in the event of a "business divorce." For instance, I once told a client, "Your brand is sizzling, but it's so widely used that the chances of trademarking it are slim to none." If you've got partners, you need to establish clear ground rules, like "If I come up with a genius idea, I own it," or "If we're in this together, then we all invest equally and share the ownership."

But here's the deal: the key is to have the conversation upfront and get everything in writing to dodge any future litigation. Trust me—I've been in the litigation trenches, and I can tell you, it's a total nightmare when things go south and those agreements aren't in place. I don't litigate anymore (been there, done that), but I've seen firsthand how quickly things can unravel without a solid plan. It's like a game of Jenga; one wrong move, and the whole tower comes crashing down.

If you're stepping out on faith to launch a business or aiming to build generational wealth through your intellectual property, you absolutely need to protect it. You want to steer clear of legal pitfalls and loopholes that could end up tightening around the brilliance of your brand like a noose. And let's be real—no one wants their hard work to be jeopardized by a lack of foresight or poor communication. Clear, upfront agreements can save you from losing your business and brand down the line.

Imagine sitting around the table with your partners, hashing out the nitty-gritty details of who owns what and how profits will be shared. It might feel awkward at first, but trust me, that discomfort is nothing compared to the chaos that can ensue if you don't have those discussions. So, grab a seat at the negotiation table, lay down the law by providing one of the agreements listed below, and make sure everyone's on the same page!

> **Partnership Agreement:** This outlines each partner's roles, responsibilities, and contributions and how profits and losses will be shared.
> **Trademark Ownership Agreement:** Clearly defines who owns the trademarks and any intellectual property created during the partnership.
> **Non-Disclosure Agreement (NDA):** This agreement protects sensitive information and trade secrets by prohibiting partners from sharing confidential details with outsiders.
> **Non-Compete Agreement:** Limits partners from starting or joining a competing business for a specified period after leaving the partnership.
> **Intellectual Property Assignment Agreement:** Ensures that any intellectual property created by a partner in the course of the partnership is assigned to the business.
> **Buy-Sell Agreement:** Establishes the process for one partner to buy out the other's share of the business if one decides to leave or if certain triggering events occur (e.g., death, disability).
> **Exit Strategy Agreement:** Outlines the process for how partners can exit the business, including valuation methods and the timeline for separation.
> **Decision-Making Agreement:** Specifies how decisions will be made within the partnership,

including voting rights and procedures for resolving disputes.

> **Investment Agreement:** Details any additional financial contributions made by partners and how those contributions will impact ownership stakes.

> **Operating Agreement:** If you're forming an LLC, this outlines how the company will be managed, the rights and duties of members, and how profits will be distributed.

By doing this, you'll not only protect your intellectual property but also foster a more harmonious working relationship among partners. Clear agreements lay the groundwork for trust and open communication, ensuring everyone is on the same page from the start. Think of it as a safety net for your entrepreneurial journey—one that can catch you before any potential pitfalls lead to costly misunderstandings or conflicts.

By addressing these issues upfront, you're setting the stage for success and creating an environment where creativity and collaboration can thrive. Don't wait for the storm to hit; instead, prepare for it now and watch your business flourish while you avoid unnecessary drama down the line!

WHAT ARE THE RISKS OF
NOT TRADEMARKING EARLY?

The biggest risk of not trademarking early is as straightforward as it gets: someone else can step in and snatch it up. That's the main issue, folks! And if that wasn't enough to get your attention, consider this: they can limit your use of the name, which can seriously put a dent in your business plans. Take Burger King, for example. Did you know the well-known fast-food giant wasn't the first Burger King? Nope! There was a small, family-run restaurant in Chicago proudly sporting that name. They didn't trademark it or consider franchising—they just viewed it as their little local gem. Enter the larger Burger King we know today, which trademarked the name and turned it into a global franchise. As a result, the original Burger King could only operate within a mere six-block radius. Beyond that, the trademark and ownership belonged to the big guys. So, if you don't protect your brand early, you risk someone else claiming it, leaving you stuck with a much smaller slice of the pie—or worse, none at all!

Another risk is your brand becoming diluted or diminished, and trust me, that's a fate you want to avoid at all costs. A perfect example to illustrate this point is the Black Lives Matter movement. Initially, there were only four individuals interested in trademarking it. They took the first steps and even filed for the trademark, thinking they were on their way to safeguarding something vital. But here's where things went sideways—they didn't follow through with the necessary legal steps. That oversight cost them dearly, robbing them of the opportunity to protect and control the use of that powerful phrase. Imagine if they had fully completed the trademark process. They would have had the legal muscle to shut down unauthorized uses and maintain ownership of a movement that resonates with millions and signifies so much.

By failing to secure their trademark properly, they left the door wide open for others to use the phrase without any accountability, potentially watering down its significance and message. It's a harsh reality: when a brand or phrase is not legally protected, it risks losing its potency in the eyes of the public.

Consider how quickly things can spiral out of control when you let others use your brand without permission. When unauthorized parties leverage your intellectual property, your brand can lose its distinctiveness and value. It can morph into something unrecognizable, and before you know it, the very essence of what made your brand unique can become muddied. This dilution can lead to confusion among consumers, who may not know which version of your brand is the real deal. Think of it like real estate. When you own property, you definitely don't want squatters—people using your space without your permission.

It's the exact same deal with your brand. If you don't protect it, others will squat on your intellectual property, and you'll lose control over it faster than you can say "trademark infringement." To avoid that headache, you might need to hire professionals or lawyers to keep an eye on your brand; otherwise, it could get diminished and lose its value.

I had a client who was all set to franchise his brand but was letting others use it without properly registering it. In legal terms, his brand was running naked—yep, that's right! It was out there, unprotected and vulnerable. Without the right protections in place, a brand running naked has no legal coverage, which is a scary thought! You need to set up the proper prophylactics—in this case, trademarks—and establish boundaries to safeguard your intellectual property. Ideally, you should secure trademarks, copyrights, and, if applicable, patents as well. It's not about randomly picking and choosing; it's about knowing which legal protections are suitable for your situation and acting on them before it's too late. Don't let your brand be the one caught with its pants down!

SMART LEGAL MOVE:
Failing to properly trademark and protect your brand isn't just a small oversight; it can lead to significant long-term consequences. By not securing your trademark, you risk opening the floodgates to dilution, misuse, and confusion. Protecting your brand early and diligently isn't just smart—it's essential to maintaining the integrity and value of your intellectual property. So, don't be like those initial Black Lives Matter founders—get your trademarks in place and keep your brand's power intact!

TRADEMARKING IN MULTIPLE COUNTRIES? IS THAT A THING?

This is especially crucial for those playing on a global stage—think fashion brands, celebrities, and influencers. What hurdles do they need to leap over, and how can they ensure their brand is protected across borders? First and foremost, businesses must understand that wherever you market your goods or flaunt your influence, that's precisely where you need to seek protection. If someone is going to swipe your brand, it's most likely to happen in the regions where your products, services, or charisma are strutting their stuff. So, the golden rule here is simple: every time you level up, you need to lawyer up.

Let's say your brand is making waves in France; guess what? You need to lawyer up in France! Or if you're making big moves in Afghanistan, that's another region where you'll need legal backup. Now, let's just say you are an author who is taking your book on a world tour—hitting the stages in France, Africa, Brazil, and beyond—you need to consider more than just your speaking points and book signings. This is the time to bring some serious legal muscle in each region.

When expanding your brand and your book is being translated into multiple languages, you're not just selling a book but sharing your intellectual property with a global audience. This means you must protect that property in every country where you're making waves. Each country operates as its sovereign entity, meaning a U.S.-based attorney can't step in and cover you everywhere. You'll need to hire legal experts who understand the specific laws and regulations in each country you're expanding. It's all about safeguarding your assets in unfamiliar territory.

In business, this is like making strategic chess moves. You have to constantly assess your position: Where are you growing, and who do you need on your team to protect that growth? Do you need a bishop to make a savvy legal move in one country or a rook to secure a different region? The bottom line is that if you're merely positioning yourself and hoping no one will snatch your brand, you're leaving the door wide open for trouble. Remember, it's not just about being proactive; it's about being smart.

When expanding into new territories, don't just think about the profits and potential market share. Consider the legal ramifications and make sure you're fully protected. Because, Darling, the last thing you want is to watch someone else capitalize on your hard work while you're left scrambling to salvage what's rightfully yours. So, get out there, level up, and lawyer up! And trust me, if you act like a pawn, others will treat you like one. You must position yourself with the right legal strategies in every territory you work in. That's how you navigate the complexities of trademarking globally—with the right team and foresight and by making sure you're protected wherever your brand is present.

Now, let me play devil's advocate here for a moment—just for the sake of education. I know some of you are reading this information for the first time and might not have done even 95% of what's covered in this book. Now, if you're not out here handling your business and find yourself tangled in a potential infringement mess, it's time to channel your inner strategist—think chess. Are you really going to throw your queen into the ring to duke it out with a pawn who might only poke their head in once or twice? I mean, come on! Your queen represents your brand, money, security, and the long-term legacy and currency you're building.

Your brand isn't just a name; it's your ticket to ride across platforms, countries, and a sea of audiences. So, you need to ask yourself, am I really about to shell out queen-level dollars for a pawn-level issue? Sometimes, the best move is to sit back and let that pawn do its thing while you keep your resources for the big players. Feel me?

But before we dive deeper, do you actually know what infringement is? Infringement occurs when someone uses your trademark, copyright, or patent without permission, leading to confusion about the source of the goods or services. It's like someone showing up at a party in the same outfit as you—awkward and unoriginal! There are several types of infringement you should be aware of:

➢ **Trademark Infringement**: This happens when someone uses a mark that is identical or confusingly similar to your registered trademark, potentially misleading consumers about the origin of the products or services. Imagine if someone started selling "Tiffany Blue" jewelry without the blessing of Tiffany & Co.—chaos!

➢ **Copyright Infringement**: This involves the unauthorized use of your original works, such as books, music, or artwork. If someone reproduces, distributes, or displays your work without permission, that's infringement. Think of all those pop songs that "borrow" from the classics without giving credit. Not cool!

➢ **Patent Infringement**: This occurs when another party makes, uses, sells, or offers to sell your patented invention without your consent. If you've invented a groundbreaking gadget and someone else is cashing in on it without your say-so, you're looking at a serious infringement issue.

But listen, I'm not saying just to let things slide without a second thought. If someone's stepping on your brand's toes, you can still hit them with a cease and desist letter, but even that needs to be done with finesse. You wouldn't send a street fighter into a boxing ring, right? For example, if the infringement is happening in the Bahamas, you can't just rely on your trusty lawyer from Philly or Chicago to handle that situation. No ma'am! You need to enlist a local attorney who knows the ins and outs of the legal landscape there.

That's like having a guide who knows the best routes through a jungle—essential for avoiding traps and getting where you need to go. So, here's what you can do if you find yourself facing infringement:

> **Cease and Desist Letter**: This is your formal way of saying, "Hey, cut it out!" It's a demand for the infringing party to stop their unauthorized use of your intellectual property. This letter should be crafted carefully, making sure to outline the specifics of the infringement and your legal rights. Think of it as your first volley in the battle for your brand.

> **Negotiation:** Sometimes, a little friendly chat can go a long way. You might be able to reach an agreement with the infringing party without escalating to legal action. A quick phone call or a well-written email can save you time, money, and a whole lot of stress. It's like a peace treaty—you can come to an understanding and move on without the drama.

> **Litigation:** If all else fails and the infringement is serious enough, you might have to take the matter to court to protect your rights. This should be a last resort because, let's face it, legal battles can be lengthy and expensive. However, if the stakes are high and your brand is at risk, it may be necessary to assert your rights legally.

Now, let's talk about strategy. You've got to think like a chess player, always two steps ahead. The key is recognizing what is worth defending and what might not be. If you're faced with an infringement that seriously threatens your brand or your bottom line, then yes, protect what's yours! That's the moment when you flex those legal muscles and show that you mean business. But if it's just a one-off incident happening in a smaller market, take a beat and think it over. Is it really worth draining your queen's energy and resources over a minor annoyance?

Sometimes, the best strategy is to save your firepower for the real challenges ahead. After all, your brand deserves to shine without getting bogged down by every little bump in the road. Focus on building your empire, securing partnerships, and expanding your reach. The world is your stage, so don't let a few pesky pawns take you off your game. Instead, invest your time and energy in opportunities that truly elevate your brand and propel you toward your goals. Ultimately, it's about playing the long game and ensuring that you're always a step ahead of the competition when it comes to your intellectual property.

SMART LEGAL MOVES REFLECTION

What unique elements of your brand, including logos, slogans, and product names, have you identified as potential trademarks, and how do they distinguish your business from competitors?

_____

_____

_____

_____

_____

_____

_____

_____

_____

_____

_____

_____

_____

_____

Have you conducted a thorough trademark search to ensure that my desired trademarks are not already in use or registered by another entity? If so, what steps will you take to address any potential conflicts?

_____
_____
_____
_____
_____
_____
_____

How will you actively monitor and enforce your trademark rights to prevent unauthorized use or infringement, and what strategies will you implement to educate your team about the importance of trademark protection?

_____
_____
_____
_____
_____
_____
_____

Legal Move #4:
Bankroll Your Brilliance
with Licensing Agreements

When you license your intellectual property, you're not giving away control—you're letting your brilliance work for you, even when you're asleep."
– Toni Moore, Esq.

Ok, let's spill the tea on contracts and licensing agreements and why they're absolutely essential for protecting your brand's assets. Imagine your brand is like a sparkling, precious, and oh-so-desirable diamond. Wouldn't you want to ensure it's locked up tight and only showcased to the right people? That's where licensing agreements strut onto the scene like the ultimate bodyguards for your brand. They're not just fancy paperwork; they're your ticket to controlling who gets to use your hard-earned intellectual property.

In the chaotic business world, where copycats lurk around every corner, having a solid licensing agreement is like having a secret weapon. It ensures that your brand remains exclusive, keeps your revenue flowing, and prevents others from misusing your name or ideas. So, buckle up because we're about to dive deep into why licensing agreements aren't just important—they're the foundation of your brand's empire!

What is a licensing agreement, you ask? Well, it's essentially permission—you're handing over a license to someone else to use what's rightfully yours. But here's the kicker: before you do that, you need to transform your brand into an actual asset with clear ownership. Otherwise, it's just an idea floating in the ether, and we all know that an idea alone isn't enough to pay the bills. Whether it's your business name, a chic clothing line, or a proprietary library of videos, it's nothing more than a concept if you don't establish ownership.

Let's break this down with a little example. Picture this: someone struts around, claiming, "Oh, I have access to a library of videos." But if they didn't license it or claim ownership, all they really have is *access*—not ownership. It's like real estate; people understand physical property, but intellectual property (IP) can be a bit elusive because it's invisible. The moment you start viewing your IP as income property, you'll treat it like the valuable asset it truly is. Once you recognize that your brand is an asset—just like a house or a car—you'll grasp the importance of controlling who gets access to it. Think about it this way: no one is just going to hand you the keys to their house unless they trust you, right? Similarly, you're not about to relinquish the keys to your brand without setting serious boundaries. I mean, I only let maybe two or three people into my refrigerator, and even then, I'm cautious about what they can snack on!

So, when you own your brand and start treating it like real property, you get to decide who gets a license to use it. It's like having a sweet ride: if you own the car, you get to choose who gets to drive it. But if you leave the keys lying around, someone else could just hop in and take off, and who knows what could happen? In the same vein, when people finally grasp that intellectual property is income property, they start realizing the necessity of controlling who gets a license to duplicate, pitch, or adapt their work. For instance, who has the license to pitch your story to a director? Who gets to turn your fabulous picture into a coloring book? It all boils down to ownership and controlling access to your invisible property.

When you start viewing intellectual property (IP) as income property, everything shifts into clarity. It's not just some abstract notion; it's real, valuable, and deserves your protection. Just like with physical property, you hold the reins on who gets a license to use it, and you have the power to hire or fire those individuals whenever you choose. That's the undeniable strength of ownership!

TYPES OF LICENSING AGREEMENTS

Now, let's talk about the different types of licensing agreements every savvy entrepreneur should know about! Licensing agreements are all about giving someone the green light to use your intellectual property—that magical, invisible asset you've conjured up from your ideas, scripts, designs, or other creative works. Once you've transformed your brilliance into a product, it's essential to establish the right licensing structures to protect your brand and ensure you're the one calling the shots.

First up, we have **exclusive licenses**. This type of agreement means you're granting one party the sole rights to use your intellectual property, and no one else can touch it.

Think of it as handing over the keys to your brand's kingdom. While this can generate some serious revenue, you're also giving away a lot of control, so choose wisely! Next, we have **non-exclusive licenses**. With this arrangement, you can allow multiple parties to use your intellectual property at the same time. It's like sharing your fabulous outfit with friends—you can all rock it simultaneously! This can be a fantastic way to maximize exposure and revenue without giving anyone exclusive rights. Then there's the **sole license**. This one is a bit of a hybrid. It gives you the right to use your intellectual property, but you're also granting someone else permission to use it. So, you get to play in the sandbox while someone else can join the fun—but no one else can. This is great for maintaining some control while still allowing others to benefit from your brilliance. Last but certainly not least, we have **territorial licenses**. This type of agreement allows you to license your intellectual property to someone in a specific geographic area. So, if you're an artist who wants to keep control of your work in one market while allowing someone else to use it in another, this is the way to go. It's like claiming your turf while still expanding your reach.

For instance, let's say you're an illustrator or a videographer hired to create a piece or a pitch deck. Sure, you want to retain ownership of your stunning work, but you also want to let someone else use it. Enter the licensing agreement! This key document sets the boundaries so everyone knows who has access, for how long, and under what conditions. Now, if you're an athlete, model, or celebrity, listen up! You need to be especially cautious about licensing your name, image, and likeness. Allowing someone to slap your gorgeous face on a product without a solid licensing agreement is like inviting trouble. The public might think you've endorsed something you haven't. So, having a license to use your identity is a must—it clearly outlines who can use your likeness, when, and for how long. And let's be real: some folks might shrug off the need for a license, thinking, "Oh, it's just a short-term gig." But that's where licensing agreements come into play! Without one, you're leaving the door wide open for complications.

If people access your intellectual property without a contract, they might try to claim joint venture status or even add their own spin to your work, turning them into co-collaborators or co-owners. I've seen this drama unfold with scripts. Someone throws in a new scene or dynamic, and suddenly, it's a full-on showdown over ownership. Without a clear agreement, you could end up in court, battling it out and potentially missing out on future opportunities because someone decided to sprinkle their creativity into your project.

Take my husband, for instance—he's a musician and always raves about synchronization rights, which are the rights to add his music to a movie or play. A sync license allows someone to use his music in their project, and it comes with royalties. That's the beauty of licensing: it lets others utilize your creation while you still cash in financially!

Now, depending on your industry, not everyone will need a license to use your work. But if your world revolves around creativity—think scriptwriting, photography, or videography—it's crucial to grasp how to leverage your intellectual property. If others want to elevate your work, you absolutely need a licensing agreement to safeguard your rights.

IS YOUR CONTRACT LEGIT?

Well-constructed contracts are crucial for a company's long-term growth and stability, serving as the backbone of your business operations and relationships. Think of contracts as the boundaries that define how you engage with everyone, from interns and associates to independent contractors. Each group must have clear guidelines detailing what they can access and what their responsibilities are. For instance, if an auditor—whether for a nonprofit or for-profit—comes knocking, they will want to review your governing documents. They'll ask questions like: Who's monitoring the work? What were the deliverables, and were they met? A contract establishes these parameters, ensuring compliance and accountability from the get-go.

To ensure your contracts are well-constructed and effective for long-term growth and stability, they should include several key components:

> - **Clear Definitions** ~ Start with clear definitions of all parties involved and any key terms used throughout the contract. This eliminates ambiguity and ensures everyone understands their roles and responsibilities.
> - **Scope of Work** ~ Specify what services or products will be provided, including detailed descriptions and any deliverables. This helps set expectations and minimizes disputes over what was agreed upon.
> - **Payment Terms** ~ Outline the payment structure, including the total amount, due dates, payment methods, and any late fees or penalties for non-

payment. This ensures clarity on financial obligations.

➤ **Confidentiality Clause** ~ Include a confidentiality agreement to protect sensitive information shared between parties. This is essential for maintaining trust and safeguarding business secrets.

➤ **Intellectual Property Rights** ~ Clearly define ownership of any intellectual property created or shared during the contract. Specify how this IP can be used and any limitations on its use.

➤ **Termination Clause** ~ Outline the conditions under which the contract can be terminated by either party. This should include notice periods and obligations upon termination, such as payment for services rendered.

➤ **Indemnification Clause** ~ This clause protects you from liability by stating that if one party is at fault for damages, they are responsible for covering those damages. Ideally, aim for mutual indemnification to protect both sides.

➤ **Jurisdiction Clause** ~ Specify the governing law and jurisdiction for any disputes that may arise. This clause determines where legal matters will be resolved, which can be crucial if parties are located in different states.

➤ **Dispute Resolution** ~ Include a dispute resolution process, such as mediation or arbitration, to address conflicts without resorting to litigation. This can save time and money.

➤ **Non-Disparagement Clause** ~ This clause prevents either party from making negative comments about the other, particularly in public forums. It protects your reputation and business interests.

➢ **Non-Competition Clause** ~ If applicable, include a non-compete clause that restricts the other party from engaging in similar business activities that could harm your interests for a specified period.

➢ **Signatures and Date** ~ Ensure all parties sign and date the contract to make it legally binding. This shows that all parties agree to the terms and conditions outlined.

➢ **Amendment Clause** ~ Include a provision that outlines how any changes to the contract will be handled. This ensures that modifications are documented and agreed upon by all parties.

➢ **Severability Clause** ~ This clause states that if any part of the contract is found to be unenforceable or illegal, the remaining parts will still be valid. It protects the integrity of the contract as a whole.

By incorporating these elements, you create a robust contract that protects your business interests, outlines expectations, and minimizes potential disputes. A well-constructed contract is not just a piece of paper; it's a strategic tool that sets the stage for successful, long-term relationships and sustainable growth.

Remember, in the game of business, your contracts are your best defense—so make them count! But it doesn't stop there. You also need to be vigilant about your external relationships. Some companies may require that you don't engage with competitors, but if you agree to that without clearly defining who those competitors are, you could find yourself out of compliance, facing serious legal and financial consequences.

I've seen these pitfalls up close and personal. One of my clients neglected to properly manage their employee benefits, and the fallout. They ended up owing the federal government a staggering $400,000. And here's a critical point: certain debts—like IRS fees, student loans, and employee benefits—are non-dischargeable in bankruptcy. This means that failing to have well-structured contracts can jeopardize your financial stability for years to come.

Moreover, consider your use of commercial credit. If you're using it for personal purchases—like buying a house but claiming it's for business—this could lead to federal investigations. Contracts must be airtight regarding what you're promising, who owns what, how payments are handled, and even things like non-disparagement. You don't want someone airing your dirty laundry on Google or Yelp because they were upset. Once something hits the internet, it can linger forever, so your contracts need to protect you from that kind of fallout.

A well-constructed contract is your shield, ensuring that nobody can checkmate your assets. It's about thinking several steps ahead, much like a game of chess. How are you positioning yourself to navigate challenges while still advancing toward your goals? How are you protecting your business as you level up and encounter new opportunities? The stronger your contracts are, the more secure your business will be as it expands.

When people like you, trust you, and see you delivering at a high level, they'll start recommending you for even bigger opportunities. I can attest to this from my own experience—coaches and clients I've worked with have returned to hire me or whispered my name to others who need legal help. But this momentum all starts with solid contracts.

So, if you're building a business—especially one designed to create generational wealth—you must ensure that your contracts are structured to support your long-term success. Remember, before you can generate wealth, you need to generate income. Contracts play a crucial role in securing that income and protecting your assets. So, take the time to craft those agreements thoughtfully; they're the foundation upon which your business will stand strong as it grows!

WHAT ABOUT CONTRACTS WHEN ENTERING PARTNERSHIPS?

When diving into partnerships, collaborations, or any kind of joint venture, let me just say it loud and clear: you absolutely need a contract—no ifs, ands, or buts about it! This isn't a game where you can cut corners. Forget about those one-size-fits-all templates that promise to magically shield you from disaster; they're about as reliable as a paper umbrella in a storm. It's not just about slapping some legal jargon together; it's about genuinely protecting yourself and your interests so you don't find yourself in a legal nightmare.

When you're teaming up with others—whether that's bringing on a partner, subcontractor, vendor, or even a sponsor—keep in mind that they're essentially putting their stamp of approval on you, and you're doing the same for them. That's all well and good when the sun is shining, but what happens when the clouds roll in? This is where the delightful concept of joint and severable liability steps into the spotlight. What does that mean? Well, it means that if things go south, both parties can be held accountable. The plaintiff doesn't just pick one; they can go after both of you. It's like a game of "Eeny, meeny, miny, moe," and trust me, you don't want to be the one they choose!

Let's say you're the one with deeper pockets—picture this: you've got $357,000 on the line. If the vendor or partner you brought in is the one who dropped the ball, the plaintiff can still decide to come after you for the whole shebang. This is precisely why doing your due diligence is an absolute must! You can't just waltz into a partnership, throwing caution to the wind and hoping for the best. Nope, that's a one-way ticket to Regret City! You need to have robust monitoring systems in place and set crystal-clear boundaries in your contracts. Even if it's just a referral, keep your guard up! I always tell my clients, "I'll happily provide you with two or three names, but the choice is ultimately yours—don't go around saying, 'the lawyer said' like I'm your personal cheerleader!" This way, you're wrapping yourself in a protective cocoon and shielding yourself from being dragged into someone else's mess.

When it comes to setting up contracts, remember this: it's not just about protecting yourself when the skies are blue and the sun is shining. Oh no, , it's about being ready for when things take a nosedive into chaos! As a former divorce attorney, I've seen it all. Relationships that start out all sunshine and rainbows can quickly turn into stormy weather. And let me tell you, when that happens, you'll be eternally grateful for those boundaries and parameters you meticulously set up to safeguard your brand. But let's be real: if you don't know what you're doing when drafting contracts related to licensing and branding, you're setting yourself up for some serious drama.

One of the biggest pitfalls? Brand ownership. We see this play out time and time again with influencers and creatives. Take Viacom, for example—no shade, but we've all watched this circus. They'll bring someone in and say, "Oh, sure, you can join our fabulous ecosystem, but guess what? We're giving you a 360 deal, and whatever you bring to the table? Yeah, we own that!" The music industry isn't any better; record companies love to let you contribute, but come album release day, they'll have someone swoop in and tweak your masterpiece. Suddenly, they're the proud parents of your creative child!

It's a bitter pill to swallow. On one hand, they're treating you like a pawn in their game of chess, but on the other, sometimes you have to sacrifice a little to get your foot in the door. Push back too hard or come off as "problematic," and you might find yourself shut out faster than you can say "contract negotiations." When you're drafting a contract, the goal is to have someone on the other side who's advocating for you. You don't want to be the one getting the short end of the stick! But if you're dealing with a company that wants to own every last drop of your creativity, like Netflix or other major players, you need to be crystal clear about what you're giving away. They're not playing "Eeny, meeny, miny, moe" with your intellectual property—they want the whole shebang!

Now, if you're licensing your brand, images, choreography, or any of your creative brilliance, that contract should be all about making the best decision for

YOU. Sure, it might feel like giving up your rights is a non-starter, but let's be real: if you're not willing to budge, you might as well wave goodbye to that deal. That's just the name of the game, especially if they don't know you, trust you, or see the long-term value in what you bring to the table. That's why I love to challenge my clients, especially those just starting out: "Can you handle this yourself? Are you ready to treat your brilliance like a business? Start your empire, earn that credit, secure that loan, and leverage yourself like Chance the Rapper!" If you can build your own brand and platform, you'll be in a way stronger position when someone comes knocking with a deal. Suddenly, you're not just a pawn; you're a player! But then the real question becomes, how much do you keep? That's where the magic of a solid contract comes into play!

But remember, the contract isn't just some magical document that gets created on the spot while you're sitting across the table or knee-deep in negotiations. Nope! Those conversations started way before you even showed up. By the time you're staring down 16 to 50 pages of legalese that looks like it was crafted by a robot, the key decisions have already been made. They might sweet-talk you with, "Oh, this is just standard and customary," but don't let that line fool you. Whoever drafts the contract holds the reins of the relationship. So, when that document lands in your hands—or pops up in your inbox—it's the result of a whole lot of prior decisions made long before you sat down to hash things out. You need to be ready to read the fine print and understand who's really calling the shots!

Now, for my legacy wealth builders, the key is knowing how to make those contracts truly work for you.

Sure, you can buy a template, but let's be real—a template is like a recipe: it's a good starting point, but it doesn't always serve up the full meal. Let me share a quick story. I once bought a yellow cake mix—not because I wanted to make a plain old yellow cake, but because I've perfected my banana oatmeal walnut bread using it. Why? Because after years of experimenting, I know exactly how much sugar, walnuts, and oatmeal to add to elevate it to pure deliciousness.

That's how contracts work! You might grab a basic template, but unless you know how to tweak it for your specific needs, you won't reap the full benefits. Just the other day, someone mentioned they were working with a client to create something valuable—intellectual property that could generate royalties—and they asked me, "How do we do that?" My answer was simple: "Hire a lawyer." You won't find the right answers online when it comes to complex deals. If you're diving into creating an IP asset and want to secure your stake, you need someone who knows the ins and outs of:

- ✓ Intellectual property law
- ✓ Brand protection and licensing
- ✓ Monitoring and leveraging your work without exposing yourself to unnecessary liability

There are countless types of contracts—affiliate agreements, influencer contracts, royalty agreements, trademark licensing, joint venture contracts—the list goes on. At one point, I tried to package these contracts together, thinking I could just hand out the yellow cake box. But what people really wanted was a custom recipe. Myron Golden once asked me, "Why are you selling all these contracts?" He got it—the real value isn't in the template; it's in the customization. I know that sometimes people may need a starter contract kit. That's why I created the Legal Box, packed with all the standard contracts you might need. But here's the crucial part: *every time* you level up, you need to lawyer up.

Not every deal can be tackled with a one-size-fits-all approach. A shopping agreement isn't going to come in a standard box of contracts, just like you won't find a wedding cake mix in your yellow cake box. It all boils down to knowing when you need customization. Different stages of business require different levels of clauses and legal expertise. So, if you're serious about ensuring your contracts are legally sound, don't just snag a template—hire a lawyer who gets your goals and can craft the agreement that will truly protect your interests.

WHAT CLAUSES SHOULD BE IN YOUR CONTRACT?

When it comes to your contracts and agreements, a few must-have clauses should make their way into almost every document, no matter the specifics. First up: a confidentiality agreement. Let's be real—if someone's stepping into your business and getting a peek at your valuable info, you definitely don't want them running around spilling your secrets like it's the latest gossip. Think of this clause as your protective shield against unwanted exposure.

Next, let's talk about brand protection. If you're putting your brand on the table, you better make it crystal clear in the contract that they don't own it! They're only getting a license to use it for the agreed-upon time, and you should lay down the law on how they can use and leverage it – no expanding or misusing your brand without having a chat with you first, got it? And then there's the all-important indemnification clause, which is like your safety net in case things go sideways. This little gem basically says, "If there's a problem and it's your fault, you're on the hook." But here's the kicker—you don't want some blanket indemnification clause that throws you under the bus just because someone else got sued. You need it to be based on actions and negligence. Ideally, go for mutual indemnification; after all, the other party could mess up, too, and you don't want to be left holding the bag!

Smart business owners know that including a jurisdiction clause in their contractual agreements is a must. This clause essentially means that if things go sideways, you'll have to duke it out in the home state specified in the contract. Trust me, having that clarity is a game-changer. I always advocate for alternative dispute resolution methods like arbitration or mediation.

As a former litigator, I've witnessed firsthand how litigation can drag on for what feels like an eternity. Lawyers can play endless games, running up those billable hours, and it can take years to resolve even the simplest of disputes. With arbitration or mediation, you could settle the whole issue in a matter of 90 days—talk about a major time-saver!

Next up, let's discuss the importance of a termination clause. You need to be covered if someone decides to bail on the agreement—whether they have a valid reason or not. Make sure you state that whatever is owed to you must be paid within 30 days of cancellation. Otherwise, you'll find yourself chasing them down for your hard-earned cash, and who wants to waste their precious time on that drama?

And let's not forget the non-disparagement clause. If the other party gets a little too emotional, they shouldn't be allowed to jump on social media, throw shade, or post defamatory comments about you. We've all witnessed celebrities airing their dirty laundry on Twitter or Instagram, and you definitely don't want your business tangled up in that kind of mess. This clause ensures that they can't bad-mouth you, whether they're on Adderall at 2 a.m. or just having a "moment." Oh wait, then there's the non-disclosure agreement (NDA), which is essential for keeping your business secrets under wraps. You don't want someone walking in, learning your trade secrets, and then running off to share them with the world. Sadly, people love to swipe ideas from others and try to compete. That's where a non-competition clause comes in handy. It prevents someone from taking your course, absorbing your strategies, and then flipping them under their own name to launch a rival business.

It's all about setting boundaries! You want to protect your business from the inside out. By establishing the right boundaries, you ensure that the people sitting at your table aren't the same ones plotting a checkmate move because they took advantage of your trust. So, take these clauses seriously and watch your business thrive without unnecessary drama!

Now, I know a lot of this may sound foreign or just like a bunch of legal jargon, but trust me when I say you have the expertise to create business opportunities that not only seal the deal but also safeguard your legacy. And that's where I come in. Let me clarify: this isn't a sales pitch. I've got clients lined up, but what I really don't want is for you to lose "it" simply because you didn't know how to secure "it."

As both a coach and a business lawyer, I've developed multiple ways for you to work with me based on your unique needs. First off, I've put together a fantastic library of template contracts in my Legally Chic Boutique— my online store where the magic happens! These templates cover everything from joint venture partnerships to licensing agreements. They're not just pulled from thin air; they're based on real contracts I've crafted for clients, all cleaned up with proprietary or personal information removed and spaces left for you to fill in your specific details—like your state or particular terms of the agreement. And the best part? These templates are available for purchase 24/7, even while I'm catching some Z's! However, if you're looking for a customized contract, that's a different ball game. I can only draft fully customized legal documents in the states where I'm licensed: Pennsylvania, New Jersey, and New York. For clients in these states, I can whip up everything from cease-and-desist letters to tailored contracts and handle all the legal tasks you need. If you're outside those states, don't fret! I can act as your legal compliance consultant or Chief Legal Officer. In this role, I take a big-picture view of your business, evaluating your brands, licenses, deals, joint ventures, and compliance needs. With over 15 years of experience in senior-level federal compliance, I know how to make sure your business is not just surviving but thriving.

I also offer a training program called Legally BYOB (Build Your Own Business). This program guides you through the essentials of business structuring, adoption agreements, licensing agreements, partnership agreements, and so much more. These aren't generic contracts pulled off the internet but crafted from my 25 years of legal experience and real-world know-how.

When you join this program, you gain access to my library of contracts, along with training videos of classes designed to help you wrap your head around the legal side of your business. And as a cherry on top, I offer discounted "Ask Me Anything" sessions where you can get personalized legal advice after completing the training. For those who complete the training, we can dive even deeper into more advanced strategies tailored to your unique situation. My mission is to make law accessible and strategic—not something to fear, but a powerful tool that empowers you to protect and grow your business.

HOW CONTRACTS & LICENSING AGREEMENTS PROTECT YOUR BRAND ASSETS

When it comes to protecting your brand assets, contracts, and licensing agreements are your best friends—think of them as the armor and shield for your business. These legal documents aren't just boring sheets of paper; they're your frontline defense against anyone who might try to sneak into your empire and claim a piece of your hard-earned success. A well-constructed contract clearly outlines who gets what, who does what, and, most importantly, who can't mess with your brand. You wouldn't let just anyone waltz into your house without knowing what they're there for, right? Contracts serve the same purpose, ensuring that every party knows their role and responsibilities like the back of their hand. This clarity fosters trust and sets the stage for successful collaborations, reducing the chances of misunderstandings down the line.

Brand assets refer to the unique elements representing your brand and contributing to its identity and value in the marketplace. These can include your logo, brand name, taglines, color schemes, packaging designs, proprietary fonts, and even the tone of your communications. Think of brand assets as the personality traits of your business—they help you stand out and communicate what your brand is all about. They're the visual and verbal cues that make your brand recognizable and memorable to consumers.

Understanding the value of your brand assets is crucial. They not only differentiate you from competitors but also create emotional connections with your audience. When consumers see your logo or hear your tagline, they should immediately think of the quality and values your brand represents. Strong brand assets can become valuable intellectual property that may generate revenue through licensing deals or increase your business's overall valuation.

Protecting your brand assets is essential because they play a vital role in your business's success. A strong brand identity helps you build trust and loyalty with your customers. This loyalty can translate into repeat business, word-of-mouth referrals, and an overall competitive advantage. When consumers associate your brand with quality and reliability, they're more likely to choose your products or services over those of competitors. Furthermore, strong brand assets create a sense of authenticity and professionalism, making your business more appealing to potential partners and investors. Additionally, brand assets contribute to your company's goodwill, a valuable intangible asset that can significantly impact your bottom line.

The goodwill generated by a well-recognized brand can lead to increased market share and premium pricing, ultimately driving higher profits. Moreover, in an increasingly digital world, your brand assets are often the first impression potential customers have of your business. A strong visual identity, paired with consistent messaging, can establish your brand as a leader in your industry and set the stage for long-term success.

Now, going back to licensing agreements, which are like the VIP passes to your brand's exclusive party when you license your brand, you're giving someone the green light to use your creative assets, but only under your terms! It's like saying, "Sure, you can borrow my favorite dress, but you better return it clean and without any drama!" A licensing agreement protects your intellectual property by laying out the rules for how others can use your brand—think of it as the ultimate set of house rules for your brand's guests. If they step out of line, you've got legal grounds to call them out and enforce your rights. Without these agreements, you're playing a risky game of trust. You wouldn't invest your money in a shady deal, so why would you let anyone use your brand without a contract? It's like giving someone the keys to your car but not asking them to sign a waiver. What happens if they crash it? Yikes!

A solid contract ensures that your brand remains yours, keeping opportunists and copycats at bay. It acts as a deterrent against misuse and helps to maintain the integrity of your brand in the eyes of consumers. So, embrace these documents as the guardians of your brand assets; they're here to help you shine without the fear of someone else snatching your spotlight. With well-crafted contracts and licensing agreements, you're not just protecting your brand—you're empowering it to soar! Here are five essential tips to help you protect your brand assets and safeguard your business for the long term:

> ➤ **Define Ownership Clearly**: Make sure your contracts explicitly state who owns the brand assets. This includes logos, slogans, and any other intellectual property. Clarity in ownership prevents misunderstandings and ensures that no one can claim your hard work as their own. When brand assets are clearly defined, it eliminates ambiguity that could lead to disputes. Use precise language that leaves no room for interpretation, ensuring that both parties are on the same page about what belongs to whom.

- ➢ **Limit Scope of Use**: When drafting licensing agreements, specify how and where your brand assets can be used. This might include restrictions on geographical locations or particular industries. Limiting the scope of use keeps your brand from being diluted or misrepresented in the marketplace. Be specific about what types of products or services can feature your brand assets, and include guidelines on how your brand should be presented. This level of detail protects your brand's reputation and ensures consistency across all representations.

- ➢ **Include Quality Control Provisions**: If you're licensing your brand, you want to maintain your reputation. Include clauses that allow you to monitor and approve how your brand assets are used. This ensures that anyone using your brand meets your quality standards, helping to uphold your brand's integrity. Consider establishing a process for reviewing materials that feature your brand, such as advertising campaigns or packaging designs. This oversight not only safeguards your brand image but also reinforces the message that you take your brand seriously.

- ➢ **Set Terms for Renewal and Termination**: Be clear about the duration of the licensing agreement and the conditions under which it can be renewed or terminated. This prevents any surprises down the line and gives you control over your brand's future partnerships. Include provisions that allow for regular reviews of the agreement to assess its effectiveness and relevance. Establishing clear termination conditions protects you from being locked into unfavorable agreements or partnerships that no longer align with your brand goals.

➢ **Implement Confidentiality Agreements**: Protect your trade secrets and proprietary information with confidentiality agreements. This ensures that anyone who works with you or licenses your brand is legally obligated to keep your business strategies and processes under wraps, safeguarding your competitive edge. Confidentiality agreements not only protect sensitive information but also build trust between you and your partners. When others know that you take confidentiality seriously, they are more likely to respect your business practices and safeguard your assets.

By following these tips, you'll not only create contracts and licensing agreements that safeguard your brand assets, but you'll also be setting the stage for successful collaborations that elevate your business to new heights. You know that feeling when you walk into a room knowing you've got it all together? That's exactly the energy you'll bring into every negotiation when your brand assets are locked down tight with clear, well-thought-out legal protections. So go ahead— put on your business armor, straighten that crown, and confidently strut into those boardrooms or virtual meetings like the boss you are. You're not just protecting a logo or a slogan; you're securing your business's identity, reputation, and future profits. Your brand deserves nothing less than the absolute best, and that means iron-clad agreements that leave no room for anyone to mess with your hard-earned legacy.

Remember, the stronger your contracts, the more solid your foundation will be as your business grows. And with those airtight legal protections in place, you can finally focus on what you do best: building your brand, leveling up, and creating the lasting legacy you've always envisioned. Don't just hope your brand survives—ensure it thrives. After all, you didn't come this far to let sloppy contracts hold you back. So let those legal docs do the heavy lifting while you shine, and watch as your brand continues to grow, knowing that every step forward is backed by strong, sassy, and savvy legal protections. Now, go conquer!

SMART LEGAL MOVES REFLECTION

What specific rights and responsibilities do you seek to establish in your contract, and how do you ensure they align with their long-term business goals?

_____

_____

_____

_____

_____

_____

_____

_____

_____

_____

_____

_____

_____

_____

_____

What risk management strategies are included in the agreement to protect your brand assets, and how can you mitigate potential legal or financial challenges?

_____

_____

_____

_____

_____

_____

_____

_____

How do you plan to monitor compliance with the terms of the agreement, and what steps will you take to address any breaches or disputes that may arise?

_____

_____

_____

_____

_____

_____

_____

_____

Legal Move #5: Uplevel Your Estate Planning

Create an estate plan to protect your reputation, goodwill, finances, and assets from lawsuits, divorces, and disputes— your legacy deserves more than a haphazard plan.
– Toni Moore

Most people avoid estate planning like it's a bad Tinder date. Why? Because it forces them to confront a truth no one wants to think about— their own death. But guess what? Just because you don't talk about it doesn't mean it's going away. In the legal world, we like to call it "legacy protection" because that's what it's really about—securing both your life's work and your legacy. Estate planning isn't just for the rich and famous; it's for anyone who doesn't want their life's work to unravel like a bad episode of reality TV. Let's be real: life is unpredictable, and as a business owner, you're not just responsible for yourself—you're responsible for the empire you're building. One moment, you're on top of the world, and the next, life throws you a curveball. I'm not just speaking from theory here. I've lived it. I was in a car accident that could've easily ended in tragedy. One wrong angle and I wouldn't be sitting here, dropping these knowledge bombs for you. That experience shook me to my core and made me realize—tomorrow isn't promised. So, let me ask you: are you leaving behind a legacy or a liability?

Here's the thing: if something happens to you, is your business going to continue thriving, or will your family be left sifting through a mess of unpaid bills, confused clients, and legal nightmares? Case in point—someone I knew passed away unexpectedly, and her family was blindsided. No plan, no instructions, nothing. Her clients started asking for refunds, demanding services she obviously couldn't deliver anymore, and her family was stuck in the middle of it. You don't want to leave your loved ones scrambling, trust me. They need to know what's going to happen to your business, how to manage it, or whether to sell it, transfer it to a family member, or maybe even put it into a trust. It's not just about passing down assets; it's about ensuring your business can live on without you.

Do you have a succession plan in place, or is it all just in your head? Spoiler alert: if it's all in your head, that's a problem. One of my clients learned this the hard way. Her husband ran their family business for years, and she wasn't involved. When he got seriously ill, she was left in the dark, having to file for guardianship just to access the business's bank accounts. Everything—from passwords to client contracts—was locked up in his mind, and without him, it was like trying to solve a mystery with no clues. All those years of building something great were on the verge of crumbling because no one else knew the playbook. So, not having a plan is planning to fail.

You've worked too hard and invested too much blood, sweat, and tears to let it all fall apart because you were too busy or too scared to think about estate planning. You need to get your affairs in order—your assets, your business, your legacy. And no, it doesn't have to be complicated, but it does have to be done. So here's what you want to consider: start asking yourself these tough questions. Who's going to run your business if you can't? Are you going to hand the reins over to a family member or a trusted colleague, or is it time to consider setting up a business trust? And if you think these questions can wait, let me stop you right there. Because that "I'll do it later" attitude is exactly how businesses turn into liabilities when their owners pass on. Don't leave your loved ones with a mountain of legal drama or, worse, an unsalvageable business.

You have the power to make sure your business thrives beyond you, to ensure that the people you love aren't left with a financial mess and unanswered questions. Estate planning is about more than just property or money—it's about continuing the legacy you've built. So yes, while it may feel uncomfortable to think about, it's a necessary move for anyone serious about their success. After all, you didn't work this hard to let it all slip through your fingers in the end, did you? No. You're smarter than that. It's time to plan like the boss you are and protect your legacy like your future depends on it—because it does. So, get out there and do the smart thing—lock down your estate plan, protect your brand, and ensure that no matter what happens, your business will thrive without you.

This isn't just about writing your will and hoping everything magically falls into place when you're gone.

We're talking cryptocurrency wallets, business accounts, real estate properties—all the things you've hustled to acquire. And believe me, I've seen firsthand how it can go sideways when no one has a clue where to find the keys to the kingdom. One of my clients inherited three properties but couldn't access a dime of them. Why? Because all the passwords were stashed on a family member's computer that no one knew how to unlock. And before you think, "Oh, I'll just reset the password," let me stop you right there—those accounts were completely wiped out. No plan, no access, no wealth. It was a disaster.

So, you really need to ask yourself: what are you actually passing down? A legacy without the assets to back it up is just a nice bedtime story. Are you giving your family something tangible—a true inheritance—or just a bunch of memories and missed opportunities? If you want to leave something meaningful, you need to leave a clear roadmap. Who owes you money? What contracts are still in play? Where are your accounts? And, more importantly, who's managing those insurance policies that could be worth millions? Because let me tell you, the bank is not going to show up at your family's door saying, "Hey, here's the $2 million we owe you in insurance!" Nope, it's up to you to make sure your family knows where to look. I know estate planning isn't a fun topic, but it's critical. At the very least, write it down. Put a note somewhere that says, "Hey, check the red book in the office for all the details." Otherwise, your family could be sitting on a gold mine and not even know it. But as a first-generation millionaire, I've put in serious work to build my wealth, but what's the point if I can't pass it down? Too many people leave money—and I'm talking serious cash—on the table simply because they didn't have a plan. No receipts, no roadmap, just chaos. And trust me, no one's going to knock on your family's door saying, "Oh, by the way, I still owe your loved one $50,000." If you don't spell it out, your family will be left in the dark, and that's a surefire way to rob yourself of the legacy you've worked so hard to create.

Estate planning is more than just a formality—it's the blueprint for ensuring your wealth, business, and hard-earned assets are passed down with legal precision. That's how you go from simply being remembered to creating a lasting legacy. So, get your plan together, lock it down, and make sure everything you've built doesn't get lost because you didn't take the time to map it all out. After all, a legacy without wealth is just another story. Don't let that be yours.

KEY COMPONENTS OF
A COMPREHENSIVE ESTATE PLAN

When we talk about an estate plan, the term alone probably makes your eyes glaze over. But listen, this is about more than just dry paperwork—it's about protecting your empire. And one of the power moves? Setting up a holding company to centralize all your assets. Whether it's copyrights, licensing agreements, real estate, or equity deals, a holding company is like the vault that safeguards your money-making treasures. These assets are the lifeblood of your legacy, and let's be honest, if you can turn it into cash quickly, it's a serious asset. Assets are the foundation of financial security, and that foundation needs to be bulletproof. Now, let's talk about your business. I know you might be running multiple ventures—some of my clients juggle 16 or 17 businesses! But here's the thing: there's a fine line between running a successful business and managing a full-blown BIZmess. And trust me, a messy, non-compliant business is nothing but a ticking time bomb. That's why I created my Do It Yourself (DIY) compliance guide, so you can figure out exactly how tight your operation is—or isn't. When I do my famous B2B Makeovers, transforming these "BIZmesses" into real, functional businesses, people are shocked to find out how much they've been getting wrong. Trust me, you don't want to be that person scrambling to fix everything after the IRS or some other agency comes knocking. Get it together now.

But hold up –the real long-term protection doesn't stop there. You've got your holding company protecting your assets and your business entity running your daily operations, but now you need to think about the future. This is where your trust and estate plan come in. This isn't just some piece of paper for the drawer—this is your legacy playbook. It ensures everything you've worked so hard to build doesn't get lost in the shuffle after you're gone. Listen, I could go on for days about wills, trusts, and estate plans (and honestly, I might—"Create Your Will Already" could be my next bestseller), but the most important takeaway is that you need a succession plan. Think of it like this: you've spent your life leaving clues for your success, but now it's time to leave blueprints for your family. Breadcrumbs won't cut it anymore. They need clear instructions, so they know exactly how to pick up where you left off, keep your wealth growing, and make sure your promises stay alive.

Here's the kicker: death shouldn't be treated like some surprise plot twist. We all know it's coming; we just don't know when. So, do you have everything in place so your family isn't left in the dark, fumbling with your business or missing out on wealth that could've been theirs? Do you have a plan that allows them to build on your success, not start from scratch? At the end of the day, a solid estate plan isn't just about passing down money—it's about ensuring your legacy keeps thriving for generations. You didn't come this far to leave your family with a mess. You're creating something lasting, something that will keep paying off long after you're gone. That's the real power of a well-constructed estate plan. It's not just about today—it's about tomorrow and every tomorrow after that.

WILLS, TRUSTS, AND HOLDING COMPANIES FOR ENTREPRENEURS

When it comes to legacy planning, too many people sleep on the details. They think a simple will is going to cut it, but that's only part of the story. A will is great for transferring assets within the first year or two after you're gone, but what happens when you have more complex plans? Maybe you want to make sure your kids aren't blowing their inheritance all at once, or you want to protect a chunk of your wealth for your grandkids when they reach a certain age. That's where a Trust comes into play.

Trusts allow you to maintain control over how your assets are distributed, especially when you don't want everything handed over all at once. You can get creative with it—phased distributions, age milestones, or setting conditions like graduation or marriage before the money flows. Now, if you've been tempted by the whole "own nothing, control everything" mentality, you're probably thinking about an irrevocable trust. It sounds sexy in theory, right? You get all the benefits, and no one can touch your assets. Except for one tiny detail—you're not actually in control of an irrevocable trust; the trustee is. So, while the concept may seem bulletproof, it comes with its own set of limitations. There's a lot of power in relinquishing ownership, but you also give up some control. That's why it's crucial to understand what type of trust fits your situation, your assets, and the legacy you want to leave.

Smart legacy planning, especially for business owners, is all about knowing how to leverage the right legal tools. Estate taxes, for instance, are an issue many people overlook until it's too late. And let me tell you, the rules are as different as night and day depending on where you live. Pennsylvania and New Jersey, for example, slap you with inheritance taxes, while New York doesn't. You've got to know the lay of the land—especially if your assets cross state lines. It's not just about leaving your business to someone; it's about minimizing how much gets siphoned off by taxes before your family even sees a dime. Here's where Trusts really shine for business owners.

Assigning your business interests to a Trust allows you to dictate how and when your family can access those assets. You can set up benchmarks—like your kids don't get full control until they turn 35 or hit certain life milestones. And if you're really on your A-game, you can even create a Trust that births another Trust—yes, a Trust that gives life to more wealth protection for future generations. Imagine setting up a fund for your grandchildren that only unlocks when they hit 21 or graduate college. That's next-level planning.

And here's a nightmare scenario I've seen too often: clients who didn't set up a Trust and ended up paying six figures in estate taxes that could have been easily avoided. Just because federal estate taxes might not apply if your estate is under $12 million doesn't mean you're in the clear. Tax laws change like fashion trends—one administration raises the exemption, and another lowers it. You've got to stay ready, and a revocable Trust can give you that flexibility. But don't get too comfortable—while a revocable Trust lets you tweak things while you're alive, it won't protect your assets if you need long-term care. Since it uses your social security number, it's still considered part of your estate and can be drained if you ever need Medicaid for long-term care.

Speaking of long-term care, Medicaid planning should be on your radar, especially if you have any family history of degenerative diseases. Medicaid has a five-year look-back period, meaning they'll review your finances to ensure you didn't try to offload assets to qualify. Understanding how both irrevocable and revocable trusts play into long-term care is essential if you don't want to burn through your assets paying for healthcare costs in your later years. But here's the kicker—it's not just about having a plan in place. Your family needs to know what assets exist and where they are. Trust me, no one's going to knock on their door with a list of your insurance policies, retirement accounts, or cash-value policies.

There's a growing trend of using life insurance policies as a way to "self-bank," creating a private financial system that can be tapped into for emergencies or investments. But if your family doesn't know that you set up one of these self-banking systems, all that planning will be for nothing.

At the end of the day, estate planning isn't just about transferring wealth; it's about making sure your family has a roadmap. You don't want them scrambling, trying to figure out what you owned, or, worse, missing out on assets that get lost in the shuffle. Success leaves clues, right? Well, you need to leave blueprints. A smart estate plan ensures that your wealth, business, and legacy continue to work for your family long after you're gone. You didn't hustle and grind all these years to leave them with a mess—they deserve the foundation you've worked so hard to build.

WILL, TRUST, HOLDING COMPANY

Now, the big question isn't just about whether you need a will, a trust, or a holding company—it's about understanding what each tool offers and how to use it wisely. If your assets don't have much value yet—and by "value," I mean real value—then all you really need is a will. It'll make sure things are sorted when you're gone without too much fuss. But if you've built up $500,000 or more in assets (some lawyers even say $1 million), it's time to step it up. A trust is your best friend at this point. Why? Because a trust offers more control—especially if you have young children, special needs family members, or, let's be real—kids you don't quite trust with a huge pile of money yet. Think back to when you were 18—would you have trusted yourself with $250,000? Exactly.

Here's another important factor to consider: your health. You know your medical history better than anyone else, and not every entrepreneur reading this is in perfect shape. But that's okay—planning accordingly is key. Many of us have life insurance policies that are gold mines for building generational wealth. That insurance payout could be the foundation your family's future is built on—and that's where a Trust comes into play. It protects and ensures that money doesn't just slip through the cracks.

For those entrepreneurs who are out here rewriting their stories—no Prince Charming needed—it's a Cinderella story of your own making. You're building wealth through sheer brilliance, but you need to safeguard it. My recommendation? Get a holding company. As a former litigator, I always think ahead: How can you make sure that if someone comes after you, your assets are untouchable? But here's the bottom line: if someone wins a lawsuit against you but all your assets are tucked away in a holding company or cleverly leveraged, they're out of luck. Sure, lawyers might use AI to dig through every nook and cranny trying to track down your assets, but if they're properly shielded, guess what? Those assets remain untouchable. And trust me, I'm always thinking 14 steps ahead of the competition when it comes to protecting what's mine. So, what's the smart move for estate planning? I've got a trifecta that'll have you covered from all angles:

- ➢ **A Holding Company**– This separates you from your wealth, giving you an added layer of protection. If someone comes after you, they'll hit a brick wall, not your assets.
- ➢ **A Will** – This is your final testament, where you leave not just your assets but your legacy. Pro tip: Use this opportunity to include heartfelt messages or

even love letters to your family. It's a beautiful way to keep your voice alive, even after you're gone.

➢ **A Trust** – Let's be honest: not everyone should get a lump sum of money all at once. You can set smart conditions, like requiring a family member to finish college, complete a financial planning course, or stay sober before they get access to the cash. You worked hard for that money—make sure it's not squandered.

And before you think it's all about control, let me clarify it's about ensuring that your legacy lasts. Did you know that 70% of first-generation beneficiaries end up bankrupting the estate because they don't know how to handle the wealth? Yep, they blow through it because no one taught them how to manage it. If you don't want your family to be part of that statistic, you need to put those boundaries in place now. That's where the holding company becomes crucial—it's asset protection 101. By separating you from your wealth, you're not just protecting yourself but ensuring your family stays safe, too. If life throws you legal curveballs, your holding company is the protective bubble your wealth sits in, untouched, ready to be passed down with precision. Bottom line: play it smart now so your legacy can thrive, not just survive.

Now, we can't discuss estate planning without diving into the intriguing world of universal life insurance. This isn't just a buzzword; it's become a hot topic among entrepreneurs looking to fund their ventures. Universal life insurance can be a powerful financial tool, but like any tool, it's all about how you wield it. This concept is beautifully encapsulated in a fantastic book called Becoming Your Own

Banker, which inspired my Legally BYOB concept. The premise is simple yet profound: you can be your own bank with universal life insurance, but you've got to grasp its different levels and nuances.

Some universal life insurance policies are as basic as they come—flat and stagnant, often failing to keep pace with inflation. Others are more dynamic and tied to stocks and bonds, which can lead to higher costs due to either active or passive management. If you're contemplating using universal life insurance as a funding source for your business, it's imperative to approach it with a strategy. You want to ensure that you're not just throwing darts in the dark but rather making informed decisions that align with your financial goals.

Here's the reality check: commercial lenders can smell entrepreneurs in need of funding from a mile away. They're poised to hit you with exorbitant interest rates— sometimes as high as 50%! However, with universal life insurance, you have a unique advantage. A portion of your premium goes into building your cash value, which you can borrow against, while another portion covers the insurance aspect. The beauty of this arrangement is that you're borrowing from yourself. But don't get too comfortable; if you die with any outstanding loans or distributions, that amount gets deducted from your policy's face value. So, while universal life insurance offers flexibility, it's crucial to be aware of its potential pitfalls. There's business credit, and then there's universal life insurance, and each has its rightful place in your financial toolbox. However, be wary of the fact that many people only sell what they know. This can lead to situations where you might be used as a pawn in someone else's hustle. Business is a game, and the pressing question is: are they genuinely helping you level up, or are they just playing you for a fool?

At the end of the day, the burning question on everyone's mind is how to tap into that money. Every financial advisor has their own hustle, but there's a stark difference between hustling big and hustling broke. Hustling big means you're playing the long game, fully believing in your vision and trusting that it will pay off in the end. On the other hand, hustling broke is a frantic chase for the next dollar or opportunity, often without a coherent strategy.

Some entrepreneurs might shy away from the insurance aspect—universal life insurance included—and that's perfectly okay. But if you're smart and strategic, remember that there's no one-size-fits-all solution in this game. The only golden rule you should adhere to? Stay legal. More legal means less stress, and when you're operating from a place of legal security, everything else tends to fall into place. So gear up, get informed, and let's make those smart moves for your financial future!

SMART LEGAL MOVES REFLECTION

How do you envision your legacy as an entrepreneur? What values or lessons do you want to pass on to your loved ones through effective estate planning?

_____

_____

_____

_____

_____

_____

_____

_____

_____

_____

_____

_____

_____

_____

_____

_____

_____

Considering the potential risks that entrepreneurs face, such as lawsuits or financial instability, how prepared do you feel your estate planning strategies are to protect your assets and ensure your family's financial security?

_____

_____

_____

_____

_____

_____

_____

How does having a comprehensive estate plan contribute to your long-term vision for your business and family? In what ways do you think an estate plan can empower your loved ones to carry on your entrepreneurial spirit after you're gone?

_____

_____

_____

_____

_____

_____

_____

Legal Move #6:
Secure Your Empire with Tax Shelters

"Protect your assets and business with smart legal moves or risk losing it all—the choice is yours."
– Toni Moore

When it comes to protecting your wealth, one of the smartest moves an entrepreneur can make is mastering tax strategy. Let's break it down: taxes are those annoying fees the government slaps on you for making money, coming in various forms like income tax, property tax, and capital gains tax—oh, joy! Your tax liability is simply the amount you owe and excessive taxation. That's when the government gets a little too greedy, taking a hefty bite out of your hard-earned cash and limiting your ability to invest, save, or enjoy the fruits of your labor. Now, navigating the labyrinth of tax laws isn't just a task for accountants in suits; it's a critical strategy that can either make or break your financial game. You don't want to be the entrepreneur caught off guard when tax season rolls around, scrambling to figure out how to pay Uncle Sam without losing your shirt. That's why you need a tax strategy that goes beyond the basics. Think long-term! This isn't just about dodging your tax bill; it's about constructing a smart, comprehensive plan that considers your entire financial situation.

Dive deep into the tax code, uncover those hidden deductions and credits, and leverage legal structures like trusts and holding companies to keep your wealth cozy away from excessive taxation. And let's be clear: we're talking tax avoidance here, not tax evasion! The former is all about using legitimate methods to keep more of your money, while the latter is a fast track to courtroom drama and serious trouble. Partnering with a tax professional who can help you navigate these waters isn't just smart; it's essential. By keeping a sharp eye on your tax liability, you'll hold onto more of your hard-earned dollars where they belong— working for you! Remember, tax planning isn't just an annual chore; it's a key component of your business strategy and levels.

PRESERVE & PROTECT YOUR WEALTH

One of the smart legal moves you can make to shield your wealth from the taxman's greedy grasp is to diversify your asset class portfolio. This means stacking your assets—those glorious things that make you money or help you pay less in taxes. And let's not forget the business entity you whip up to pass on that generational wealth like a family heirloom! Now, some folks might raise an eyebrow at this suggestion, but hear me out: creating a nonprofit can be your golden ticket. Not only do you get to do good in the world, but you can also slash your taxable income while you're at it. Funnel up to 50% of your taxable income into your nonprofit and watch the magic happen. Plus, you can hire your kiddos and family members, all while keeping the funds in line with your mission. Why toss your hard-earned cash to some faceless charity when you can build something that reflects your values?

If a nonprofit doesn't tickle your fancy, how about throwing some cash into donor-advised funds? This nifty little fund allows you to earmark money for future charitable donations and score an immediate tax deduction. Or consider a nonprofit lead or remainder trust, which lets you allocate funds for causes that matter to you while also protecting your wealth and deducting it from your taxable income. Let's talk retirement plans, shall we? I know, I know—retirement isn't the hottest topic, but trust me, the earlier you start saving, the better off you'll be! Why wait until you're well past your prime to start raking in the dough? The power of compounding interest is the real deal. Ever heard of the Rule of 72? You divide 72 by your interest rate and boom—that's how long it'll take for your money to double!

If you have a solo 401(k) or a self-directed IRA, you're on your way to letting that cash grow like a champ. And here's a juicy pro tip: self-directed IRAs let you invest in your friends' businesses, real estate, or other ventures, all tax-deferred until you cash out in retirement. Talk about playing the long game with Uncle Sam!

While we're on the topic of long-term investments, if you're eyeing real estate or other assets, don't sleep on the 1031 exchange. A 1031 exchange, named after Section 1031 of the U.S. Internal Revenue Code, is a tax-deferral strategy that allows an investor to sell an investment property and reinvest the proceeds into a new property while deferring capital gains taxes on the sale. This strategy is often used in real estate investing to allow for the continuation of investment growth without the immediate tax burden that typically follows the sale of an appreciated asset.

Key Features of a 1031 Exchange:

> ➤ **Like-Kind Property:** The properties involved in the exchange must be of "like kind." This generally means they should be similar in nature or character, but they don't have to be identical. For example, you can exchange a residential rental property for a commercial property.

> ➤ **Investment or Business Properties Only:** The exchange must involve properties held for investment or business purposes. Personal residences and properties primarily for personal use do not qualify.

> ➤ **Timelines:** There are strict timelines associated with a 1031 exchange:
> > ○ Identification Period: You have 45 days from the sale of your property to identify potential replacement properties.
> > ○ Exchange Period: You must complete the purchase of the replacement property within 180 days of the sale.

> ➤ **Qualified Intermediary:** To facilitate a 1031 exchange, you must work with a qualified intermediary (QI). The QI holds the sale proceeds until you are ready to purchase the new property, ensuring that you don't take actual possession of the funds.

> ➤ **Tax Deferral, Not Elimination:** It's important to note that a 1031 exchange defers taxes rather than

eliminates them. When you eventually sell the new property without another exchange, you will owe taxes on the capital gains.

➢ **Boot:** If any part of the transaction involves cash or non-like-kind property, it is referred to as "boot." Boot is taxable to the extent of the gain realized.

Benefits of a 1031 Exchange:

➢ **Tax Deferral:** Allows you to defer paying capital gains taxes, which can significantly enhance your cash flow for reinvestment.

➢ **Leverage:** You can leverage the proceeds from the sale of your property to acquire a more expensive property, potentially increasing your investment portfolio.

➢ **Diversification:** It provides an opportunity to diversify your investments by exchanging one type of property for another.

In summary, a 1031 exchange can be a powerful tool for real estate investors looking to defer taxes while reinvesting in new properties. However, just a little reminder: hold onto those assets for at least a year to avoid getting slapped with ordinary income tax rates. Wait it out, and you'll get taxed at the more favorable capital gains rate. Thinking about deferring some income? Check out 409A plans for a deferred income structure, which allows you to stash away some of your earnings for later, all while keeping Big Brother at arm's length—because who wants to give away more than they have to? Just remember, this isn't a DIY job; you'll want a pro by your side to steer you clear of penalties while maximizing your benefits.

Here's another cheeky strategy: hire your kids! Yes, even the little ones can help you whittle down your taxable income—whether they're helping out in your business, modeling for your brand, or raking in royalties for their creative work. Just keep that paperwork on lock because the IRS loves to play detective.

LEGAL SIDEBAR To summarize, here are some key strategies to protect your wealth from excessive taxation:

> ➤ **Diversify Your Asset Classes:** Stack up those money-making assets across various classes, from real estate to stocks, and consider business entities that facilitate generational wealth transfer. This diversified approach not only cushions you against market volatility but also optimizes tax advantages that come with different asset types.
> ➤ **Create a Nonprofit:** Establishing a nonprofit organization allows you to do good in the world while significantly reducing your taxable income. You can funnel up to 50% of your taxable income into your nonprofit, thereby lowering your tax liability. Plus, you can hire family members to work for the organization, ensuring that funds are used to support a mission that resonates with your values rather than handing them off to an unknown entity.
> ➤ **Consider Donor-Advised Funds:** Investing in donor-advised funds lets you set aside money for future charitable donations while enjoying an

immediate tax deduction. This flexible option enables you to decide when and how to distribute funds to your favorite causes, allowing you to control your charitable giving strategy.

➢ **Utilize Retirement Plans:** Don't underestimate the power of retirement planning! The earlier you start saving in a solo 401(k) or self-directed IRA, the more time your money has to grow through the magic of compounding interest. You can contribute to these plans tax-deferred, allowing your investments to flourish without the burden of immediate taxation.

➢ **Engage in 1031 Exchanges:** When it comes to real estate investments, consider a 1031 exchange, which allows you to defer taxes on the sale of a property by reinvesting the proceeds into another similar property. This strategy helps you keep your money working for you while navigating the complex world of real estate taxation. Just remember, patience is key; holding onto the property for at least a year can land you a more favorable capital gains tax rate.

➢ **Implement Deferred Income Structures:** Exploring options like 409A plans can be a game-changer for deferring a portion of your income. This strategic move allows you to control when you're taxed, optimizing your financial situation for future growth. However, this isn't a one-size-fits-all solution, so enlisting a professional to guide you through the complexities is essential.

➢ **Hire Your Kids:** Don't underestimate the power of involving your children in your business! Whether they're helping with administrative tasks, modeling your products, or earning royalties for creative contributions, hiring them can help reduce your taxable income. Just make sure you document everything to keep the IRS happy and ensure compliance.

Remember, the one who earns is the one who gets taxed, and that's just the way the cookie crumbles. But listen up! There are ways to shift income or rights to other entities, like a trust or nonprofit, that can lighten that tax load while preserving wealth across generations. Feel me? When we talk about preserving wealth, it's all about using some slick legal strategies to minimize your tax liabilities. You might hear folks throw around terms like "tax shields," but let's cut to the chase: we're talking about tax deductions, loopholes, and smart financial moves that let you keep more of that hard-earned cash in your pocket. One way to do this is by assigning your trust as a member of your S-Corp or LLC. Yep, you heard that right—a trust can actually be a member of your business entity!

This little trick allows you to shift your interests and protect assets for the next generation. It's like putting your wealth in a protective bubble! This approach doesn't just shield your wealth; it brings your family into the game. You can train them in financial literacy, give them hands-on experience managing wealth, and even hire family members to work for you. Think about it: you can offer employment benefits and maximize tax advantages to keep that wealth flowing within the family. Everyone wins, and you're leveraging the tax code like a pro!

Now, let's talk about those tax shields. Many people overlook the perfectly legal loopholes and deductions just waiting to be snatched up. Take the 529 plan, for example. It's a tax-advantaged savings plan designed to encourage saving for future education costs. You can stash away money for your children or grandchildren, and even if they decide college isn't their jam, that money can still be used for other qualifying expenses. It's a fantastic way to maximize deductions while saving for the future.

Oh, and don't sleep on retirement plans for your kids! That's right—even minors working for you can have a Roth IRA or a 401(k). By directing a portion of their earnings into these accounts, you're not only creating long-term wealth for them but also enjoying a sweet tax deduction for your business. It's a total win-win!

Now, let me spill some tea about a strategy that blew my mind. One family set up a family business entity with ten family members all in on the action. They didn't just stop there—they took out life insurance policies on each family member (paid for by the family trust), then borrowed against the cash value of those policies. With that money, they bought hotels! Talk about building wealth! They were leveraging life insurance, business protections, and the power of family teamwork all at once. That's how you play the long game in wealth protection.

At the end of the day, it's about knowing the system, leveraging those loopholes legally, and building structures—whether it's trusts, insurance policies, or business entities—that work together to create a multi-generational wealth strategy. You've got to think ahead, plan strategically, and make sure your family is along for this fabulous ride!

LEGAL STRUCTURES AVAILABLE FOR BUSINESS OWNERS TO REDUCE TAX LIABILITIES

When we're talking about tax shields (or, as I like to call them, tax reduction strategies), we're really diving into the fabulous world of reducing your taxable income, lowering your effective tax rate, or even deferring or eliminating certain taxes. Now, don't get it twisted—I'm not trying to get sued here, so let's make sure we're on the legal side of things, alright? Tax shields or shelters—whichever flavor you prefer—can help you keep more of that hard-earned cash, but we've got to play by the rules!

Self-Directed IRA

Let me tell you about one of the most powerful tools in your tax-saving arsenal: the self-directed IRA. This is a total game-changer! With a self-directed IRA, you aren't limited to the usual boring investments. Nope! You get to dive into a world of exciting possibilities. You can invest in all kinds of ventures, even something as unique as a ski resort! It lets you invest in other people's businesses or even in some unique ventures, like a ski resort! I had a client who took the plunge and invested in a ski resort through his self-directed IRA. And guess what? It was 100% legit! As that investment started raking in the dough, he kept reinvesting those profits, letting his money do some serious overtime. That's the kind of smart, legal move that makes your dollars work harder than a personal trainer!

A self-directed IRA puts you in control, allowing you to grow your wealth on your terms. If you're tired of watching your money sit around doing nothing while it could be working for you, the self-directed IRA is your key to unlocking financial freedom! Just remember to play by the rules and consult with the right professionals. We're all about keeping things smart and fabulous!

Hiring Your Family as Independent Contractors

Now, how about hiring your family or friends as independent contractors? Seriously, if they're already enjoying the fruits of your labor and dining at your table, you might as well put them to work, right? It's a win-win situation! By hiring them to tackle legitimate tasks—whether it's helping with social media, managing your calendar, or even assisting at events—you can write off those expenses as business deductions. Now I get it: not everyone's cut out to be a boss, but that doesn't mean your loved ones can't lend a helping hand to keep your business running smoothly. Imagine the synergy! You're not just handing out cash; you're building a family empire while keeping your financials in check. Plus, it's a fabulous way to bring your crew into the entrepreneurial fold and teach them a thing or two about hard work and business savvy.

And let's not forget those sweet tax benefits! When you pay your family or friends for their contributions, you get to keep more of your hard-earned money in your pocket. It's like having your cake and eating it too! Just make sure you keep everything above board—document what they're doing and how much you're paying them. After all, the IRS loves paperwork, and you want to keep them happy while you reap the rewards of your savvy business moves. So go ahead, tap into that family talent pool, and let them help you build your empire while enjoying the perks of working together!

Donor Advised Funds

Now, let's spill the tea on donor-advised funds. This strategy is a powerful way to reduce your taxable income while supporting charitable causes. You can stash away money in a donor-advised fund for nonprofit purposes, and whatever amount you contribute is tax-deductible. Yes, you heard that right! This financial tool allows you to give back to the community while keeping some of those hard-earned dollars out of Uncle Sam's greedy hands. Here's how it works: you set up a donor-advised fund, which acts as your personal charitable fund. You make a contribution to it, and voilà! You get a nice tax deduction for that year.

Then, you have the freedom to recommend how that money is distributed to various charitable organizations over time. This means you can be strategic about your giving—supporting the causes that truly matter to you without feeling rushed. But wait, it gets even better! With a donor-advised fund, you can invest those contributions, potentially growing the fund over time. This creates an even bigger impact when you eventually distribute the funds. So, if you want to make a difference while making smart financial moves, consider hopping on the donor-advised fund train. You get to contribute to causes you care about, and your money continues to work for you. It's a solid win-win!

Tax Deferral Strategies

And don't forget about tax deferral strategies! This is where the magic happens. You can defer hefty sums of income—think $100,000, $200,000, or even more—and put that cash to work for you instead of handing it straight to the IRS. Imagine using that deferred income to scoop up additional assets or investments that can generate even more income down the line. It's like getting a financial power-up that lets you level up your wealth while dodging that tax hit for a little longer.

For instance, you might consider strategies like 401(k) plans or other retirement accounts that allow you to contribute pre-tax dollars. This means you're not just saving for your future; you're also reducing your current taxable income, which is a double win! You can also look into certain types of insurance policies that allow for tax-deferred growth. The beauty of these strategies is that they give you time to grow your investments without the immediate pressure of taxation, allowing your money to compound and flourish.

So yes, there are plenty of tools at your disposal, but it all comes down to knowing how to legally leverage these strategies to cut down on your tax liabilities and grow your wealth like a boss! Don't just let your money sit there; make it work for you! Embrace these strategies, consult with financial pros who know the ins and outs, and watch your wealth soar. After all, in the world of finance, it's not just about how much you make but how much you keep!

SHOULD I BE HANDLING MY OWN TAXES?

There's an old saying in law school: "A person who represents themselves has a fool for a client." And let me tell you, that wisdom extends to entrepreneurs who think they can juggle everything—especially when it comes to taxes and wealth protection. Most entrepreneurs are juggling a million things at once. We're hustling with sales and marketing and trying to figure out the latest TikTok trends or

Instagram algorithms. On top of that, we manage clients, coaching programs, and contractors. Now, throw navigating tax laws into that mix. Honey, that's a recipe for disaster!

One of the biggest mistakes entrepreneurs make is believing they can handle all the legal and tax matters themselves. But here's the kicker: tax laws and regulations are constantly evolving! For instance, did you know that the Required Minimum Distribution (RMD) for retirement used to kick in at 70½ years old and is now 72? That's just one tiny example of how the rules shift, and if you're not keeping up, you could face penalties for not adhering to the latest guidelines.

Another common pitfall? Not grasping the crucial differences between being taxed as an S Corp versus a C Corp or even understanding how different tax rules apply to an LLC. You need to nail these details from the get-go because if you don't, and an audit comes your way, the IRS doesn't care if you were clueless—they'll still hit you with penalties for mistakes. If you present incorrect information, they might even see it as fraud, even if it was just an honest mistake. Trust me, you do not want that label. That's when you're dealing with more than just the IRS; you could find yourself face-to-face with the Attorney General's office or even the U.S. Marshals!

Let's not forget another major mistake: many entrepreneurs fail to keep track of where their money is coming from, where it's going, and what expenses are being deducted. This can lead to significant problems. I've seen far too many people mix personal expenses with their business accounts. When you do that, you're co-mingling your finances, which signals to an auditor that you're treating your business like an extension of your personal life. Once they catch wind of that, they'll treat your business as an "alter ego," meaning they can hold you personally liable for any business issues. And darling, that's a position you do not want to find yourself in!

So, if you're an entrepreneur thinking you can just "wing it" with taxes, remember: the law doesn't care about what you don't know. Those mistakes could end up costing you big time.

Overall, as you level up in your business, it's essential to lawyer up and plan strategically—especially when it comes to taxes. Now, while I'm not a tax attorney, I've worked with enough clients to know the ropes, and I know when to refer you to a tax professional who specializes in this arena. Here's the scoop: long-term tax planning isn't merely about paying taxes; it's about strategically using the rules, deductions, and loopholes available to reduce your tax liabilities while protecting your assets.

One piece of advice I always share with my clients— especially those in family businesses or partnerships—is to be cautious when signing tax returns, particularly if you're married. There's a little something called "innocent spouse relief," and while I'm not suggesting you should be thinking about divorce, but if you can't trust your spouse with financial matters, don't just sign off on a tax return because they said so! If something's amiss on those forms, you could be held liable, too. Trust me, you want to steer clear of any unnecessary tax trouble.

Now, I don't delve too deeply into the tax side of life, but here's what I do know: long-term tax planning is all about understanding debits and credits and leveraging the rules to your advantage. For instance, many entrepreneurs are so caught up in their hustle that they forget to track their expenses properly. I hear folks say, "I'm just saving receipts," but, Honey, there are smarter ways to handle this!

Personally, when I travel for work, I don't waste my time hoarding every single receipt like a squirrel with nuts for winter. Nope! I give myself a fabulous $100 per diem and make sure it's accounted for in my planning. You need to know the rules and—more importantly—how to use those rules to your advantage for the long haul. Planning is key not only to reducing your tax liabilities but also to securing the future of your business and protecting that beautiful empire you've built. So, ditch the receipt hoarding and start working smarter, not harder!

Remember, it's not just about reducing taxes; it's about using the tax code to maximize your business's growth and protect your personal assets. The worst mistake entrepreneurs can make is neglecting to pay taxes or underestimating the importance of tax planning for their business. So let's get serious about this—your financial future depends on it!

SMART LEGAL MOVES REFLECTION

How well do you understand the tax implications of your current wealth management strategies? What steps can you take to educate yourself further on how taxes may impact your assets and overall financial plan?

_____
_____
_____
_____
_____
_____
_____
_____
_____
_____
_____
_____
_____

What specific strategies have you considered or implemented to minimize your tax burden? How do you assess their effectiveness in protecting your wealth from excessive taxation?

_____

_____

_____

_____

_____

_____

_____

In what ways do you think proactive tax planning can influence your long-term financial goals? How can creating a robust estate plan help you safeguard your wealth for future generations while minimizing tax liabilities?

_____

_____

_____

_____

_____

_____

_____

Legal Move #7: Regulations You Can't Afford to Ignore

Stay ahead of regulators like the IRS and SEC to avoid legal trouble—never forget compliance is currency
– Toni Moore

When people think of "losing it," they often picture lawsuits or tax issues coming in like a dramatic plot twist to take down their business. But let me drop a truth bomb: the real landmines are those regulators lurking in the shadows, just waiting to blow up everything you've worked so hard to build if you're not paying attention. In this chapter, we'll shine a spotlight on the following regulators: the Internal Revenue Service (IRS), the Department of Labor (DOL), the Securities and Exchange Commission (SEC), the Federal Trade Commission (FTC), and the Financial Crimes Enforcement Network (FINCEN). And let's not forget about the lesser-known but equally formidable forces—Divorce Court, Orphans' Court, and Surrogacy Court. Each of these regulatory bodies and courts plays a crucial role in maintaining order, fairness, and compliance in their respective areas. Ignoring their regulations can lead to severe consequences, including legal penalties, financial loss, and damage to reputation. Understanding their functions is essential for entrepreneurs to navigate the business game successfully.

Internal Revenue Service (IRS)

The IRS is the federal agency responsible for administering and enforcing the Internal Revenue Code of the United States. Its primary duties include collecting taxes, processing tax returns, and enforcing tax compliance. The IRS ensures that individuals and businesses pay the correct amount of taxes based on their income, deductions, and credits. It also provides guidance on tax regulations and can impose penalties for non-compliance.

Department of Labor (DOL)

The DOL oversees federal labor laws related to employment, wages, and working conditions. It enforces regulations concerning minimum wage, overtime pay, workplace safety, and employee benefits. The DOL also handles issues related to workers' rights and investigates complaints regarding unfair labor practices, ensuring that employees are treated fairly and compensated appropriately.

Securities and Exchange Commission (SEC)

The SEC regulates the securities industry and protects investors by enforcing securities laws. Its mission includes maintaining fair, orderly, and efficient markets. The SEC requires publicly traded companies to disclose financial information and adhere to rules that promote transparency and accountability in financial reporting. It also investigates securities fraud and other violations of securities law.

Federal Trade Commission (FTC)

The FTC is tasked with protecting consumers and promoting competition. It regulates advertising and marketing practices, ensuring that businesses do not engage in deceptive or unfair practices. The FTC also oversees mergers and acquisitions to prevent monopolies and promote healthy competition in the marketplace. Its primary focus is consumer protection and maintaining a fair business environment.

Financial Crimes Enforcement Network (FINCEN)

FINCEN is a bureau of the U.S. Department of the Treasury that combats money laundering and other financial crimes. It collects and analyzes information about financial transactions to identify and prevent criminal activity, such as terrorist financing and tax evasion. FINCEN also enforces compliance with anti-money laundering laws and works with financial institutions to ensure they report suspicious activities.

Divorce Court

Divorce Court deals with legal disputes arising from the dissolution of marriages. This court handles the division of marital assets, including businesses, real estate, and financial accounts. In addition to asset division, it also addresses issues like child custody, alimony, and child support. Divorce Court ensures that the rights of both parties are protected during the separation process.

Orphans' Court

Orphans' Court is responsible for overseeing the administration of estates, particularly when a person dies without a will (intestate). It determines the distribution of the deceased's assets and handles matters related to guardianship for minors and the management of trusts. The court ensures that the wishes of the deceased, as outlined in a will (if one exists), are carried out and that the assets are properly managed.

Surrogacy Court

Surrogacy Court oversees legal matters related to surrogacy agreements, including the rights of intended parents and surrogates. This court ensures that the surrogacy process complies with applicable laws and protects the interests of all parties involved, particularly the children born through surrogacy. It often addresses issues related to parental rights, custody, and the enforcement of surrogacy contracts.

They can snatch away your business, your retirement plan, and even your legacy if you don't play by the rules. These agencies aren't here for a casual chat about your latest brilliant idea or innovative venture—they're all about compliance, transparency, and protecting the public interest. If you think you can skate by with a "who, me?" attitude, think again! They're watching from the shadows, ready to pounce the moment they catch a whiff of any shenanigans. These regulators have a laser focus on making sure everyone plays fair in the sandbox. They're not just checking boxes; they're enforcing the laws that keep the business landscape stable and equitable. Whether it's monitoring your tax filings or ensuring your labor practices are up to snuff, these watchdogs are relentless. They have the power to throw the book at you, and trust me, you don't want to be the one they make an example of.

So, if you're thinking about cutting corners or ignoring the fine print, remember: these agencies don't play games. They'll swoop in and take everything you've worked for in the blink of an eye, leaving you scrambling to pick up the pieces. It's a tough love kind of reality check, but the stakes are high, and you have to stay sharp if you want to protect your empire.

Now, let's take a stroll down the celebrity case files, shall we? Look at some of the richest, most successful entrepreneurs who thought they were untouchable—only to face the music when they ignored regulatory forces. From the infamous tax evasion cases that landed big names in hot water to the shocking compliance failures that drained fortunes, it's clear: respect these regulators or risk losing it all. The moral of the story? You might be a genius in your field, but if you don't keep your eye on the compliance ball, you could end up losing everything faster than you can say "audit." So, stay sharp, stay informed, and remember, when it comes to regulations, ignorance is not bliss—it's a fast track to disaster!

IRS: You Can't Hide from the Tax Man:

➢ **Case in Point:** Lauryn Hill, the Grammy-winning artist and entrepreneur, had a moment of major oversight when she decided to ignore her tax obligations on her income between 2005 and 2007. Spoiler alert: that little tax oversight landed her in the slammer for three months in 2013 and knocked a whopping $1 million off her fortune. Ouch!

➤ **The Lesson:** As entrepreneurs, we often juggle income streams from multiple sources, making tax filings feel like trying to solve a Rubik's Cube blindfolded. But here's the kicker: the Internal Revenue Service regulates how you report and pay taxes on every single dollar you earn. Miss a beat, and you're not just looking at back taxes—you could find yourself sporting a criminal record. And let's be real: you can't build generational wealth from behind bars. So, keep your financial ducks in a row, or you might just find yourself singing a different tune about compliance!

DOL: Labor Laws Don't Care About Your Bottom Line

➤ **Case in Point:** Kim Kardashian's SKIMS brand found itself in hot water with the Department of Labor over factory labor violations. Talk about a wake-up call! While Kardashian's company scrambled to fix the issues, it served as a major reminder for all entrepreneurs about the importance of accountability in business.

➤ **The Lesson:** The Department of Labor isn't playing around when it comes to regulating wages, overtime, and working conditions. So, if you think outsourcing labor or using contractors gives you a free pass, think again, darling! You can still be held accountable for violations, even if they happen halfway around the globe. Ignore labor laws at your peril—your business could face hefty fines, shutdowns, or a reputation in tatters. Keep your eyes wide open, or you might find yourself on the wrong side of a scandal!

SEC: Watch What You Say When Money's Involved

➢ **Case in Point:** Elon Musk's infamous 2018 tweet declaring that Tesla had "funding secured" to go private turned into a fiery debacle with the Securities and Exchange Commission. He ended up getting slapped with a $40 million fine and was stripped of his chairman title. Ouch!

➢ **The Lesson:** The SEC is not messing around when it comes to public financial disclosures. Whether you're raising funds from investors or just sharing your latest business milestone on social media, remember: every word counts, honey! One misleading statement—whether you meant it or not—could land you in hot water with fines, penalties, or worse, losing control of your own company. So, think twice before hitting send; your empire depends on it!

FTC: Transparency Is Not Optional

➢ **Case in Point:** Health brand Teami and celebrity influencers Cardi B and Jordin Sparks found themselves in a sticky situation when the Federal Trade Commission (FTC) came knocking for not disclosing paid endorsements on social media. Teami ended up shelling out a whopping $1 million fine, and those influencers had to scramble to amend their posts. Talk about a PR nightmare!

➢ **The Lesson:** The FTC is serious about regulating advertising and marketing, especially when it comes to consumer protection. Whether you're an influencer or an entrepreneur using endorsements to boost your brand, transparency is a must—no ifs, ands, or buts! If you think you can skate by without disclosing sponsorships, think again. The FTC won't hesitate to come after you with fines that can seriously slice into your profits. Keep it real, and keep your wallet intact!

FINCEN: Follow the Money or Pay the Price

➢ **Case in Point:** DJ Khaled and Floyd Mayweather found themselves in hot water with the Financial Crimes Enforcement Network (FINCEN) for promoting cryptocurrency investments without properly disclosing their payments. Khaled ended up coughing up $150,000, while Mayweather wasn't off the hook, shelling out a staggering $300,000 in fines. Ouch!

➢ **The Lesson:** FINCEN means business when it comes to regulating financial transactions and enforcing anti-money laundering (AML) efforts. If you're raking in large sums, especially in the wild world of crypto, you better make sure you're following the rules. Failing to disclose your transactions or adhere to AML regulations can lead to serious penalties—or worse, criminal charges. So, keep your financial game on point and don't let the regulators catch you slipping!

Orphans' Court, Surrogacy Court & Register of Wills: Don't Let the Courts Control Your Legacy

➢ **Case in Point:** When Prince passed away without a will, his $300 million estate spiraled into chaos faster than you can say "Purple Rain." The Orphans' Court had to swoop in to figure out who his heirs were, resulting in a long, drawn-out, and costly legal battle. Talk about a royal mess!

➢ **The Lesson:** Entrepreneurs are often laser-focused on building their wealth, but planning for what happens after you're gone is just as crucial. The Orphans' Court and the Register of Wills are ready to regulate the distribution of estates when there's no clear plan in place. If you skip out on drafting a solid will, be prepared for your assets to get stuck in court for ages, with legal fees devouring a chunk of your hard-earned money instead of passing it on to your loved ones. Don't let your legacy be a cautionary tale—get your affairs in order!

Divorce Court: When Business and Personal Life Collide

➢ **Case in Point**: When Jeff Bezos and MacKenzie Scott decided to call it quits in 2019, Scott walked away with a jaw-dropping 25% of Amazon's stock, worth a cool $36 billion. Sure, Bezos kept the voting control, but let's be real—the financial and reputational fallout was monumental.

➢ **The Lesson**: Divorce Court doesn't mess around when it comes to dividing marital assets, and that can include your precious business. If your company was launched or flourished during your marriage, you could find yourself sharing more than just your heart. Protect your interests with a prenuptial or postnuptial agreement, or you might end up watching your empire crumble while your ex cashes in. Don't leave your future to chance—get that paperwork in place!

Remember, the law is much like a jealous mistress. She might not be the most glamorous of companions but trust me; when she feels disrespected or neglected, her wrath will explode. You don't want to be caught in the fallout when she decides to unleash her fury, leaving everyone in her path scrambling to pick up the pieces and bowing down to her demands. So, give her the attention she deserves—because if you don't, you'll find out just how fierce she can be!

THE SMART LEGAL MOVE: RESPECT THE REGULATORS

Listen up, because this is where the rubber meets the road! Each of these regulators is in place to enforce laws that protect consumers, employees, and investors alike—and trust me, they don't discriminate between celebrities and everyday entrepreneurs. You might think you can pull a fast one or sidestep their rules, but let me tell you, that's a surefire way to find yourself in hot water. Ignoring these regulatory bodies or, even worse, trying to outsmart them can cost you not just your business but potentially your freedom and future. These agencies are like the watchful guardians of the marketplace, ensuring everyone plays by the rules. They're not here to crush your entrepreneurial spirit; they're here to keep the playing field level. So, if you think you can just skate by without following the rules, think again. The consequences can be severe—fines, penalties, or even the dreaded shutdown of your business. The truth is that many entrepreneurs underestimate the power these regulators hold, and that's where the real danger lies.

Imagine waking up one day to find that your business is under investigation for something you thought was no big deal. It happens more often than you think. Take the celebrity examples we've discussed—each one thought they could navigate the waters without a life jacket, only to find themselves drowning in legal fees and public scrutiny. You don't want that to be you! So, what's the next Smart Legal Move you need to make to protect your business, brand, and bank? It's time to roll up your sleeves and get savvy about compliance.

Start by familiarizing yourself with the regulations that apply to your industry, from labor laws to advertising standards. Don't just skim the surface, dive deep! Make it a point to stay updated on changes in laws and regulations that could affect your business. Consult with legal experts who can help you navigate the often-murky waters of regulatory requirements. Think of them as your legal lifeguards—ready to rescue you from potential drowning in red tape. They can help you set up compliance protocols and ensure that you're not only meeting the minimum standards but exceeding them. By staying informed and proactive, you'll not only safeguard your assets but also set yourself up for long-term success.

And let's be real: respecting the regulators isn't just about avoiding trouble; it's about building a solid foundation for your business that can weather any storm. It's about establishing trust with your customers and partners, showing them that you operate with integrity. When you make it clear that you take compliance seriously, you're sending a strong message that you're not just another fly-by-night operation. So, take that leap—embrace compliance and turn those regulations into your secret weapon! Instead of viewing regulatory requirements as obstacles, see them as stepping stones to building a resilient, reputable, and successful business. After all, the road to entrepreneurial success is paved with smart decisions and respect for the rules of the game.

CONTACT KEY REGULATORS

In the world of entrepreneurship, navigating the rules and regulations set by various governmental bodies is crucial for the success and longevity of your business. Ignoring these regulators can lead to severe consequences, from hefty fines to the loss of your business altogether. This section provides an overview of essential regulatory agencies and where to find more information. Familiarize yourself with these entities to ensure compliance and protect your hard-earned legacy.

> ➤ Internal Revenue Service (IRS) ~ Website: www.irs.gov
> ➤ Department of Labor (DOL) ~ Website: www.dol.gov
> ➤ Securities and Exchange Commission (SEC) ~ Website: www.sec.gov
> ➤ Federal Trade Commission (FTC) ~ Website: www.ftc.gov

➢ Financial Crimes Enforcement Network (FINCEN)
~ Website: www.fincen.gov

SMART LEGAL MOVES REFLECTION

Now that you know the importance of staying informed about industry regulations, what steps will you take to enhance your knowledge and ensure compliance in your business practices?

_____

_____

_____

_____

_____

_____

_____

_____

_____

_____

_____

_____

_____

_____

Now that you know the potential risks associated with ignoring regulations, how will you prioritize compliance in your business strategy to safeguard your assets and reputation?

_____

_____

_____

_____

_____

_____

_____

Now that you know the significance of conducting regular compliance assessments, what specific actions will you implement to evaluate and improve your adherence to necessary regulations?

_____

_____

_____

_____

_____

_____

The Smart Legal Conclusion

First, thank you from the depths of my entrepreneurial soul for grabbing a copy of "DON'T LOSE IT!" You've just taken a significant step toward not just surviving but thriving in the thrilling (and sometimes chaotic) world of entrepreneurship. As you flip towards the last page, I want you to pause and reflect: What have I learned? Are you empowered to take those essential legal steps to protect your business? Have those lightbulbs gone off, highlighting how crucial it is to integrate legal strategies into your entrepreneurial business?

Now, I know this was a legal overload, but let's face it—navigating the legal landscape is as essential as knowing your product inside and out. You wouldn't go into battle without armor, would you? Think of it this way: the legal info is your protective gear. The lessons we've covered in this book aren't just theoretical fluff; they're the lifelines that will keep your business afloat when the waves get rough.

Now, let's rewind and spotlight some of those essential legal moves, shall we? Because let's face it—if you're going to build a fortress, you need to know what the foundation looks like.

➢ **Formalize Your Business:** If you haven't taken this step yet, I'm looking at you with a raised eyebrow! Setting up a formal business entity isn't just about waving a fancy paper around; it's about protecting yourself from liability. You want a strong structure that lets you scale without sweating bullets over every little hiccup.

➢ **Own Your Intellectual Property:** You are a creative genius—own it! That intellectual property of yours is worth its weight in gold. Don't let anyone saunter away with your ideas like they're going out of style. Understand what you have and protect it like it's your most prized possession because it is!

➢ **Trademark Your Brand(s):** You want your brand to be as unique as your morning coffee or favorite drink. So why not ensure no one else can take a sip? Trademarking isn't just a legal formality; it's your golden ticket to brand ownership, ensuring you can strut your stuff without worrying about someone else cashing in on your brilliance.

➢ **Take Charge of Your Licensing Agreements:** Your brand is your baby, and it deserves top-notch protection. Proper licensing agreements aren't just nice to have—they're essential! Think of them as guardians who serve as gatekeepers for your business, brand, and bank.

➢ **Uplevel Your Estate Planning:** This isn't just about passing down wealth; it's about making sure your legacy shines bright. A solid estate plan means your vision persists, even if life throws you a curveball.

Don't let your hard work go to waste because you didn't take this seriously!

➢ **Secure Your Empire with Tax Shelters:** Let's be honest, taxes can be a major buzzkill. But with the right strategies, you can navigate the tax landscape and keep more of that sweet cash in your pocket. Who doesn't want that? Think of it as building a moat around your financial fortress—keeping those pesky tax monsters at bay.

➢ **Respect the Regulators:** Compliance is like that friend who keeps you grounded when you start floating away. You need them in your life! Staying on top of regulations ensures your business runs smoothly and protects you from costly fines that could drain your coffers faster than a bad investment.

So, what's the bottom line? Building a financial fortress isn't just a nice-to-have; it's an absolute must if you want to financially secure your future through entrepreneurship. Moreover, making smart legal moves is your golden ticket to navigating the entrepreneurial landscape with confidence and flair. So, think of this book as a blueprint that helps you create a foundation that you build upon throughout your lifetime.

As you now realize, building a financial fortress is not a set-it-and-forget-it exercise that you do one time. Integrate these legal tools into your operations and watch as your confidence soars and your entrepreneurial journey transforms into a powerhouse of wealth and security. And don't forget to bankroll your brilliance! The value you bring to the table is extraordinary—don't underestimate it. Make smart legal moves that ensure your genius translates into financial success. Your legacy is worth more than just a pretty portfolio or a pile of bills. Please don't leave it to chance; secure it with savvy legal strategies that will protect your hard work and pave the way for a prosperous future—today, tomorrow, and forevermore.

Thank you once again for trusting me to be part of your journey. Now go out there and build that fortress—your life, lifestyle, and legacy deserve it!

About The Author

With over twenty-five years of distinguished experience in the legal field, Toni Moore, Esq., LLM, CEBS stands as a formidable authority in navigating complex legal landscapes. She is the founder of Moore Legal Firm, established in 2000, and has built a reputation for her strategic foresight and comprehensive legal expertise. Toni's career spans diverse specialties, including family law, probate administration, business law, intellectual property protection, business succession planning, employee benefits compliance, and estate protection.

Toni's educational background is both extensive and impressive. She holds a Bachelor's degree in American History from the University of Pennsylvania, a Juris Doctorate from Temple Law School (1998), and a Master's in Taxation from Temple Law (2006). Her commitment to advancing her knowledge is matched by her dedication to her clients, evidenced by her membership with the Pennsylvania Bar Association and the New Jersey Board of Bar Examiners since 1999. Toni's career began at the law offices of Marks & O'Neill, where she honed her skills as a business lawyer and defense litigator. Her journey continued with the U.S. Department of Labor in 2005, where she worked closely with business regulators and investment bankers, refining her expertise in asset protection, financial security, and business compliance assessments.

In 2011, Toni pivoted her focus from corporate law to fostering relationships with emerging entrepreneurs, reimagining and expanding Moore Legal Firm into a boutique practice dedicated to safeguarding the interests of high-profile clients and ambitious entrepreneurs. Her client roster includes notable figures such as Darrin P. Hensen, Kim Sledge, Charron Monaye, Ms. Evelyn Braxton, and Tiffany "The Budgetnista" Aliche. Beyond her legal practice, Toni is a bestselling author, with titles including Handle Your Business: Power Moves to Make Your Dreams a Reality, Uplevel Your Life, The Unapologetic Guide to Manifesting Success, Boss Up!: Upgrade Your Mindset to Uplevel Your Success and Stop Being a Doormat and Start Being a Boss: How to Stop Doubting Yourself and Start Living the Life You Want.

Her work reflects her unwavering commitment to empowering individuals and businesses to navigate legal challenges with confidence and foresight. Toni Moore's career is a testament to her strategic acumen and dedication to her clients, making her a trusted advisor and a leader in the legal community.

www.ingramcontent.com/pod-product-compliance
Lightning Source LLC
Chambersburg PA
CBHW071227210326
41597CB00016B/1976